Praise for Jose Canseco's *Juiced*

"A dash of realism and candor."

—*Boston Globe*

"What I want to know about Jose Canseco is, how come I still like the guy so much? No, I'll go even further: I admire him . . . he is a rogue, and genuine rogues are rare, inside baseball and out."

—Michael Chabon, author of
The Amazing Adventures of Kavalier & Clay

"A compelling, quick, fun read . . . [Canseco] is a kind of folk expert on steroid use and abuse."

—Salon.com

"[*Juiced* is] riveting testimony, not from a lab technician, university professor, or union lawyer, but from a real-life case study."

—*Sports Illustrated*

"A sweeping indictment . . . and a real scream."

—Slate.com, A Best Book of 2005

VINDICATED

VINDICATED

BIG NAMES, BIG LIARS, AND
THE BATTLE TO SAVE BASEBALL

JOSE CANSECO

SIMON SPOTLIGHT ENTERTAINMENT
NEW YORK   LONDON   TORONTO   SYDNEY

Simon Spotlight Entertainment
A Division of Simon & Schuster, Inc.
1230 Avenue of the Americas
New York, NY 10020

First Simon Spotlight Entertainment hardcover edition April 2008

SIMON SPOTLIGHT ENTERTAINMENT and colophon are trademarks
of Simon & Schuster, Inc.

For information about special discounts for bulk purchases,
please contact Simon & Schuster Special Sales at 1-800-456-6798 or
business@simonandschuster.com

Designed by Nancy Singer

Manufactured in the United States of America

10 9 8 7 6 5 4 3 2 1

Library of Congress Cataloging-in-Publication Data
Canseco, Jose, 1964–
   Vindicated : big names, big liars, and the battle to save baseball /
by Jose Canseco.
       p.   cm.
   1. Canseco, Jose, 1964–   2. Baseball players—United States—
Biography.   3. Doping in sports.   4. Baseball.   5. Baseball players—
United States.   I. Title.
   GV865.C313A3 2008
   796.357092—dc22   2008003449
   [B]

ISBN-13: 978-1-4165-9187-0
ISBN-10:   1-4165-9187-7

CONTENTS

VINDICATED

1

THE GODFATHER
OF STEROIDS

In early February 2005, some years after I left Major League Baseball, I was getting ready to launch a second career, this time as a writer. My debut book, *Juiced: Wild Times, Rampant 'Roids, Smash Hits, and How Baseball Got Big,* was about to be published, and I guess I was as excited as any first-time author. Maybe *more* excited, to be honest, because I had some pretty controversial things to say about the game, and I knew I was about to really stir things up. In the book, I admitted that I had been a frequent user of anabolic steroids, a performance-enhancing drug, and I made no apologies for it. I said that 80 percent of my fellow players also did steroids, and I named names: Mark McGwire, Jason Giambi, Rafael Palmeiro, Ivan Rodriguez, Juan Gonzalez, and others.

I talked about how I taught many of the guys, named and unnamed, everything they needed to know about steroids, and said I shared my knowledge freely as I moved from one team to the next. Whenever anyone wanted to know anything about steroids, he always got the same answer: "Talk to Jose. Jose knows. Jose's your man." So they came, and talked, and asked questions. And I shared everything I knew, with friend and foe alike.

"The first thing you will notice is an increase in strength," I would tell them. "But you won't see much difference at the beginning. You'll feel it, though, and that'll give you a psychological edge. Then, in about four or five weeks, you'll start seeing some real, physical changes, and at that point, hell—the sky's the limit."

I was like a goodwill ambassador, the Godfather of Steroids, and I was genuinely glad to be of help. Why? Because I was a huge fan of the stuff. I thought steroids were the future. As far as I was concerned, steroids were a miracle drug, and I thought *everyone* should be on them. You could build strength, heal faster, and live longer. You'd have to be crazy *not* to try them.

Did I think I was giving away some kind of trade secret? Was I worried about helping the other guys, guys who would compete against me on the field or try to take my job? Hell, no! Steroids didn't make me a great baseball player. I was *already* a great player. Steroids simply gave me an edge, physical and psychological, and I loved that about them. I loved the whole idea. So I spread the wealth. I was happy to do it. I wanted to share and I did so hundreds of times, too many times to count.

A couple of weeks before my book was scheduled to appear, I got a call from HarperCollins, the publisher. One of the names I was naming had to go, they said. That name was Roger Clemens.

"Why?" I asked. I didn't understand. This guy was a huge star. He belonged in the book.

They didn't have an answer. I asked my agent. He didn't know. My manager didn't know either. And the publisher couldn't, or wouldn't, explain it to me. I asked my book editor, the publisher herself, even the publisher's attorney—no one could give me a decent reason.

Still, Roger Clemens was effectively excised from my book. One of the greatest players of all time, and what I really wanted to say about him and steroids was taken out of my book. Somebody, somewhere, had decided, for reasons that were never fully explained to any of us, that Roger Clemens, arguably the greatest pitcher in Major League Baseball history, seven-time winner of the Cy Young Award, the reigning Cy Young champion, was not going to be connected, in any way, to the steroid scandal.

"But why?" I protested. "All I said is that I thought Roger *might have* been dabbling. It's not like the other guys, the ones I saw with my own eyes."

Nobody knew why. That was essentially the answer: *We don't know.*

If there was a lesson to be learned from the experience, it was a pretty simple one: that stuff about the truth setting you free? It's bullshit.

I thought back to some of the lighter moments I'd shared with Roger over the years. I would hit a 500-foot homer, and his head would snap back in wonderment and awe. "Man!" he'd say. "You must have had your juice this morning!" One day, in the field, he took a look at the veins popping out of my arms, big as plow lines, and he shook his head in amazement. "I bet if I sliced that vein, Deca would fly out and hit me in the face!" (He meant Deca-Durabolin, a tissue-building steroid that manages to keep swelling to a minimum.)

On other occasions, casual as you please, Roger might say, "I think I need a B-twelve shot right about now." And off he'd go into the sunset. I didn't follow him into the sunset, or into the locker room, for that matter, but at the time I figured he was going off to juice up. That was the way baseball players commonly referred to steroids, as B_{12}. On the other hand, for all I knew, Roger really *was* a fan of vitamins.

"I still don't get it," I said. "Why can't I name Clemens, when I can name all the other guys? Don't they believe me?"

"No, no, no," my lawyer told me. "They believe you. They know it's just you and a guy in a room, your word against his, which is the case with all of these players. But with Clemens, well—it's different."

"How is it different?"

"We don't know, Jose. It just *is*, okay?"

"No, it's not okay. I'm not claiming I saw him juice up. I didn't. I'm talking about connecting the dots, about an educated guess."

"Well, I guess it still bothers them. You're implying that

he might have taken steroids. They don't like it, and it's not going in the book."

That made no sense at all. None of it made any sense, on any level, but I couldn't do anything about it. Roger Clemens was out, and no amount of arguing was going to change that. The "offending" sections were removed, and the book quickly marched toward publication.

At that point, it was time to start the press junket. My first stop was New York City, to meet Mike Wallace and the *60 Minutes* crew. They were waiting for me in a spacious loft in downtown Manhattan, empty except for a couple of chairs. As soon as they got the lighting figured out, the cameras began to roll. I looked at Wallace and plunged right in. I told him about my book, I told him about steroids and how they had taken over the game. I told him how I thought the owners had condoned steroids because they made the game more exciting and sold more tickets. I told him I used steroids while I played. And I named names. *Again.* I went through all the same names I'd mentioned in the book, including the one name the publisher had left out: Roger Clemens.

I admitted to Mike that I had never seen Clemens shoot up, but that I had my suspicions. All those Cy Young Awards. The way he was throwing, hard and fast and steady, without seeming to break a sweat. The way he seemed to be getting stronger as he got older. What else could it be? Good genes? Hell, while most of Clemens's peers were sitting on porches, in rocking chairs, with old dogs at their feet, he was still pitching rockets.

I went on to tell Wallace that I was a fan of steroids, within reason: "I truly believe that because I've experimented with it for so many years that it can make an average athlete a superathlete. It can make a superathlete incredible; just legendary." I also told him that I didn't think I would have hit 462 home runs or become the first player to hit 40 homers and steal 40 bases in the same season, back in 1988, if I hadn't juiced up. But you still needed talent. Steroids couldn't do anything for you if you didn't already have talent.

When Wallace asked me if I was ashamed of what I had done, I was honest about that, too: "That's a tough question. I tried to do everything possible to become the best player in the world. Do I believe that steroids and growth hormones helped me achieve that? Yes. Were there a lot of players doing it that I had to compete against? Yes."

I guess I never answered the question, so maybe I should try to answer it now. I wanted to be the best baseball player in the world. That was my goal, my only goal, really, and I never let things stand in the way of my goals. So in that sense, no, I'm not ashamed of it. I cared so much about winning, and about making the game more exciting for the fans, that I did what I had to do. Let's face it, when people come to the ballpark, or watch us on TV, they want to be entertained. I took steroids to make myself the greatest entertainer I could be, and that didn't seem like too high a price to pay.

Wallace went back to the names. I told him that I, personally, had injected Mark McGwire, and that I'd counseled Jason Giambi on the proper use of steroids. I also described Giambi as "the biggest juicer in baseball."

I talked about Rafael Palmeiro, Juan Gonzalez, and Ivan "Pudge" Rodriguez, juicers all. I had injected each of those men myself, on numerous occasions, and I had also watched them do the deed themselves.

"And what you're doing to baseball now—you're taking on the whole establishment?" Wallace asked.

"I don't know if I'm directly trying to take on the whole baseball establishment," I replied. "I'm just basically telling the story of my life."

"How much of your entire career's success do you attribute to the use of steroids?"

"Maybe not accomplish [*sic*] the things I did, the freakish things I did. [But] who knows? A lot of it is psychological. I mean, you really believe you have the edge. You feel the strength, and the stamina." This is exactly what I always told my fellow players when they asked me about steroids. The psychological edge is a huge component. You believe in steroids to such a degree that it changes the way you play. Confidence is a huge part of the game. Confidence intimidates your opponents. And it could be argued that the psychological benefits are even more significant than the physical.

Wallace went on, "Did you give some of the steroids to other players?"

"Not mine, no. No. Did I put them in contact with people to acquire them? Yes. Did I educate them on how to use them properly, in what way, shape, or form, and when, and with what supplements? Yes. Absolutely."

When the cameras stopped rolling, Wallace asked me if we could talk, off camera. He kept me there for another hour, clearly curious about steroids. He had more questions, and more *intelligent* questions than I'd heard in the years of counseling my fellow players. He wondered how the steroids and human growth hormones (HGH) might help him, a man in his eighties, live a longer, healthier life. He wanted to know everything. How long it took for the drugs to kick in. The potential side effects. The effects on mental clarity. How they made you feel. How they made you look—could they change your face? He was hungry for information, and he'd come to the right guy: the Godfather of Steroids. I answered every question, and I did it gladly. Everyone is interested in living longer and living better.

When Wallace was done interrogating me, I could see I had piqued his interest. Whether I'd made a convert of him, I can't say. Still, I know I was pretty convincing. I'd had this same conversation hundreds of times before, with hundreds of baseball players, and most of them had gone on to become users. Does that make me a bad person? I don't think so. An informed user is a smart and happy user. I was just the guy with the recipe, the man with a map to the Fountain of Youth.

The next thing I knew, even before the *60 Minutes* interview had aired, someone leaked a copy of my still-unpublished book to the *Miami Herald*. As you might expect, all hell broke loose. It was the biggest story of the week. Television, newspapers, magazines, radio—everyone was talking about my book. The *Miami Herald*, the newspaper that leaked the story, described me as the "NotCredible Hulk," and the book was dismissed as "the ravings of a vindictive, attention-starved, has-been 'roidhead."

They said I wrote the book to make a "fast, dirty buck" and called me "Monica Lewinsky with a bat." Monica Lewinsky? Really? I didn't realize she'd been lying.

A reporter noted, "The claimant has so little credibility as to render any charge immediately suspicious."

I was prepared for some criticism, but I had also expected, maybe naively, that some people would see the good I was trying to do, would understand that I was trying to shed some light on the sorry state of baseball. After all, every word in my book was true. Was it so hard for so many to face the truth? I guess so.

Rafael Palmeiro was the first player to take a swing at me. He'd heard that I'd named him in the book, identifying him as a user, and he was pissed. "I categorically deny any assertion made by Jose Canseco that I used steroids," he said in a prepared statement. "At no point in my career have I ever used steroids, let alone any substance banned by Major League Baseball."

Sure, Rafi. And I never cheated on anyone.

Tom Verducci of *Sports Illustrated* added fuel to the fire by saying that I had "the kind of credibility not even nanotechnology could find or measure," then added, "[Canseco] needs the money and the attention, and he has no friend or future in baseball, all of which make him highly toxic as a reliable source. He is easily dismissed."

Sure, I made money on the book. I'm happy to admit that. But is that a crime? This great country was built on the profit motive. And anyway, I had motivations beyond the financial ones: I wanted the truth to get out. The truth about the players. About the drugs. About the bosses, who knew exactly what was going on. And about the game's uncertain future.

But I also wrote the book for another reason, and maybe I'm a fool to admit it, but I'll admit it because it's the truth: I wrote *Juiced* to get back at Major League Baseball for blackballing me and booting me from the game. I loved baseball in ways the guys who ran the show would never understand; ways they *couldn't* understand. I wrote my book to let them know that they couldn't destroy lives with impunity. Not just my life, but the lives of plenty of other players. And I wrote it because I had an important story to tell, and I wanted the world to hear it.

Now that the story had leaked, I began getting calls from reporters around the world, but I couldn't talk to any of them until after the *60 Minutes* piece had aired, which wasn't scheduled for another couple of weeks. Not that I was so eager to talk to them, especially in light of the media's early response—insults and accusations and name-calling.

As the anti-Jose storm continued to rage, Harper-Collins—in an effort to minimize potential damage from the leak—was scrambling to move up the publication date. They also approached *60 Minutes* about possibly running their interview a week earlier. Luckily, the folks at CBS thought that was a wise idea, and they made the necessary adjustments to the schedule.

The following Sunday, the day before the book was released, the interview with Mike Wallace aired. I thought the piece looked pretty good, except for one huge, glaring omission: Roger Clemens wasn't mentioned. That part of the interview had ended up on the cutting-room floor. Once again, Clemens had dodged the bullet.

"Why?" I asked my team—publisher, agent, lawyers, managers. "How did this happen?"

The answer was always the same: "Hell if we know."

Someone then suggested that maybe the *60 Minutes* producers hadn't felt safe using Roger's name, since it had been excised from the book. I didn't understand why that mattered. Those guys loved controversy. Why would they shy away from it?

Someone then suggested that Roger might be working with investigators to blow the lid off this whole sordid steroid scandal. Roger Clemens as an undercover agent? I didn't think so.

Finally, I came up with a theory of my own. It's a little far-fetched, admittedly, but I'm a bit of a conspiracy nut, so bear with me: Roger Clemens was from Texas. He went to play for the Astros, to be close to his family. George W. Bush, a former owner of the Texas Rangers baseball team, is, like Clemens, a proud Texan. Clemens is a personal friend of Bush Sr. and his wife, Barbara. Clemens still has a standing invitation from Bush Jr. to visit the White House anytime. Getting the picture? Maybe the president of the United States, or his daddy, the ex-president, made some calls and took care of things for good ole Roger.

I'm not saying this is a *fact*, but, as conspiracy theories go, it was as good as any, because clearly something strange was happening here.

With the *60 Minutes* interview out of the way, I now faced two entire weeks of press to push the book, and I've got to tell you—I wasn't looking forward to it. I would be doing nonstop interviews with hundreds of reporters who were all gunning for me. Where's the fun in that?

The *Today* show was first in line, and they wanted to do a pre-interview, so I grudgingly agreed to suffer through it. I took the call in my car, en route to the airport, and the woman on the other end had no tact whatsoever. She was aggressive in the extreme, asking every dumb question in the book: "Did you do the book because you're broke?" "How did you blow all those millions of dollars?" "Are you still doing steroids?" "What does it feel like, ratting out all of your old friends?"

Why didn't she ask me any questions about the stuff in the book? I was telling the world that 80 percent of the guys on the field were doing steroids, and that the bosses knew but were reluctant to ruin the party by actually doing something about it. Why didn't we talk about that? It's one thing for a reporter to think I was a rat, or to think I was only doing the book for money, and a reporter is of course free to ask me anything he or she wants to ask, but there's a diplomatic way to phrase even the most insulting questions. How about one intelligent question for every shameless attack question? No, I guess that was too much to ask.

She wasn't done yet and I was already fuming, so I told

her I'd call her back. I immediately speed-dialed my agent and lit into him, saying I didn't appreciate the way these people were treating me. He did his best to calm me down, assuring me that the actual *Today* show interview would be much friendlier and far more professional, but at that point I was beyond listening. I took the next exit, turned the car around, and headed home. *Fuck this,* I thought. *Fuck everyone. I'm not doing this.* Let the media go after someone else.

I got home and locked myself up in the house. I didn't leave for an entire week. Everyone was calling—my agent, managers, reporters, friends, family—but I didn't give a damn. What was the point of telling the truth when it was obvious these media people couldn't handle the truth? They didn't care about the truth. Why had I bothered to write the book? Didn't anyone realize that I was trying to do some good for baseball? Sure, names were named, and that had to hurt, but it wasn't my job to protect the guilty. And without names, did I even have a book? Would a publisher even print it? The clear answer was no. When I was in New York pitching the book to publishers, the first thing every single one of them wanted to know was "Are you naming names, and what names are you naming?" They made it clear from the beginning: no names, no book. So I named some names. More important, I revealed the long-hidden fact that baseball had fostered an environment where steroids were not the exception but the rule; where a player *not* on steroids was the freak; where four out of every five players were on performance-enhancing drugs. *That* was the story. That was the *point* of the story.

Predictably, the press did what it always does: instead of looking at what I'd written, they dismissed the book out of hand. Most reporters had only two basic questions for me: Why do you lie? How big was your advance? Needless to say, this was not a lot of fun. I had expected some criticism, sure, but I hadn't in my wildest dreams imagined that the message would be completely ignored (or worse).

That same week, the week the book was released, Jason Giambi held a press conference at Yankee Stadium, where he said that everything I had written about him was a lie. "I think it's sad," he said. "He's delusional." Then Mark McGwire gave a statement to *60 Minutes*, denying he had ever used steroids: "Once and for all, I did not use steroids or any illegal substance. The relationship that these allegations portray couldn't be further from the truth."

Relationship? I never said McGwire was a friend. I said we'd juiced up together. Plain and simple.

Even Tony La Russa, my old manager from Oakland, went on the offensive. "It's a fabrication," he told Mike Wallace. "First of all, I think [Canseco's] in dire straits and needs money. I think secondly it's a healthy case of envy and jealousy."

He also said that when I had played for Oakland, I would laugh about the many hours the other guys were spending in the gym, saying I didn't have to work out because I had my "helper. . . . He was having help in a different way. You know, the easy way." La Russa had much more to say about me, and I thought he sounded a little like an aggrieved ex-wife. He tried to make me look as bad as possible, while proudly supporting his other players. He said I had physically "changed. . . . [He] got bigger than ever, and the coaches and I got suspicious and actually confronted him."

Dave McKay, an Oakland coach from 1984 to 1995, was quoted on the same subject, *me*, by the *Toronto Sun*. Apparently I had told him—even though I didn't remember telling him—that I had discussed steroids with hundreds of players, and that all of them invariably got around to the same question: "I won't get too big, will I?" I think that's a question well worth asking, mind you, particularly given the subject.

After La Russa's informative chat with *60 Minutes*, he went on to write an editorial for the *San Francisco Chronicle* in defense of his big friend, whom he had managed in both Oakland and St. Louis. "Mark McGwire's historic career did not involve the use of any illegal or unethical performance-enhancing substances," he said. "Canseco's credibility has steadily declined to the point of zero with his latest accusations concerning McGwire and his A's teammates during the 1987–1995 period."

Sure. Okay. If you say so. McGwire was being celebrated as the best slugger of the modern era, if not the best ever, but he didn't get any help from steroids. As the guy who actually jammed the steroid needle in McGwire's ass, the bullshit was really burning me up.

By then I'd had a full week to cool down, and I was tired of the negative spin, so I decided I should answer my agent's call and get the media tour rebooked. It was time to get out of the house and deal with the press. It was time to tell my side of the story. I was kind of hoping that most of the press had cooled off, too, and that maybe some of them would be open to the possibility that I'd been truthful in my book. Alas, that wasn't in the cards. Most reporters had pretty much written their story before they even talked to me, and the interviews invariably had the same negative tone. It was a foregone conclusion: *Jose Canseco is a rat and a liar*.

"If I'm lying," I would say, "let's see the lawsuits. I named names. If I'm not telling the truth, don't you think these guys would be coming after me? If someone was lying about me, I know I'd go after them."

No answer. Just silence. No one was taking my side.

On one occasion, a reporter just kept trying to push my buttons, talking about my "outrageous fabrications" and whatnot, and I almost lost it. "You don't know me," I said, barely contained. "You don't know anything about me. Have I ever lied to you? Do you have 'sources' who have a problem with my credibility? You treat me as if I've been telling lies all my life, and you judge me, and you're basing that on what, exactly?"

That wasn't the problem, though. The real problem was that the reporters didn't *want* to believe me. If I had said three or four players in the entire league were dabbling in steroids, *maybe*, but I was saying that four out of five guys were juicing up: *80 percent of the entire league*. It was the truth, and I'll say it again: the press couldn't handle the truth.

One reporter simply refused to accept it. "If these outrageous allegations are actually true," he said, "why don't we have the story?"

"Why? I'll tell you why: because you haven't been doing your jobs."

The idiots. I was *giving* them the story, but they couldn't see past their own ignorance to accept it as truth. They were also seriously biased. They didn't like me, so they didn't believe me. (They didn't like Roger Maris, either, and during his quest in 1961 to break Babe Ruth's single-season home-run record, they openly hoped that Maris would fail.) McGwire, on the other hand, was a big, lovable lug, and big, lovable lugs always tell the truth, right? So McGwire they believed.

The fans didn't seem to have a problem with me. Whenever I showed up for a book signing, there were lines out the door. This was in late February, and it was incredibly cold on the East Coast, but they still waited in long lines for hours and hours for a chance to walk away with a signed copy of my book. That was a pretty good feeling. From time to time, though, I wondered if some whackjob might show up with my book in his hands, then curse and spit in my face. But that never happened. The people who came out to see me were never less than fully supportive.

Wait. That's not entirely accurate. Back in March, if I remember correctly, less than a month after the book was released, my lawyer and I were at a signing at a Sam's Club in Tampa, and everything went well. Met a lot of fans, sold a lot of books. On our way out, however, I saw this guy in his midthirties, carrying a sign. It said CANSECO IS A TRAITOR AND A LIAR, or words to that effect.

We ignored him and tried to walk out to the car, but he dropped the sign and came at me, and my lawyer, Rob Saunooke, stepped between us and knocked the son of a bitch to the ground. (In case you're wondering, Rob is bigger than I am.) The guy sat there looking at us, not getting up, maybe *afraid* to get up, but he was screaming: "You suck, Canseco! Every word you write is a lie! Your whole fucking life is a lie!"

Instead of sticking around for the rest of the crazy man's show, we hurried outside and got into our car. "Did you see that guy's face?" I said, upset. "He was so full of hate! What is that shit?"

"Forget about it, Jose," Rob said. "You can't make everybody happy."

"I don't give a damn about making people happy. I just don't understand people like that. I'm just telling the truth. It's not my fault if he doesn't like what I have to say."

"The world is full of idiots," Rob said. "You know that."

It still rankled. Every word in *Juiced* was true. Then again, as I'd already learned, the truth didn't set you free.

On our way back to the hotel, we stopped for a bite to eat. Rob could see that I was still pissed, and in the middle of the meal he put his fork down and tried to help me snap out of it. "You know, you're not upset about that idiot back there," he said. "You're upset about all the idiots in the media who have been so ridiculously relentless in their attacks."

"No, I'm not," I said.

"My advice is to forget them. All of them. The best thing you can do, the only thing you can do, is to keep telling your story, keep getting the truth out."

"Yeah, yeah. Fat lot of good that's going to do me."

He took another bite, swallowed, and stared across the table at me. "I'm going to tell you something, Jose," he said finally.

"It sounds like you're winding up for one of your lectures."

He ignored me. "One of the most amazing things about you, to me, is that you never listen to advice, not to mine and not to anyone else's."

"It's usually bad advice."

"You always do exactly what you want to do."

"That's right, I have to live my own life. Make my own mistakes."

"And the amazing part, as I was saying, is that you never stop believing you can do whatever you set your mind to do."

"Been that way since I fell in love with baseball."

"If I told you tomorrow, 'Jose, you can't climb Mount Everest,' you'd say, 'Bullshit, I'll be ready in six months.' "

"And I would be."

"I know you would. And that's one of the things I like about you. If you believe in something, you don't let anything stand in your way. You just go out there and make it happen. I don't think I've ever met anyone with that kind of faith and determination and unquestioned belief in their own ability."

"Yeah, I'm pretty optimistic."

"*Optimistic* doesn't even begin to describe it," Rob said.

"What's your point?"

"Just that you should forget this negative stuff. One day, you'll look back on this and laugh. One day, you'll be the guy everyone remembers as the first one to stand up and pull the covers back on the bastards at Major League Baseball."

But I wasn't laughing the next day, or the day after that.

In fact, in the weeks ahead, some of that universal goodwill from the fans that I'd experienced at the beginning of my book tour had dissipated, probably as a result of all the bad press, and, on more than one occasion, I'd be approached by an unhappy baseball fan who would question my honesty and my motivations. I was always surprised that the littlest guys were generally the most aggressive. It's as if they wanted me to get mad, wanted me to throw a punch. But I never did. I kept cool. And if I felt I couldn't keep cool, I'd walk away.

Then it was time for my ESPN interview with Pedro Gomez, one of their on-air reporters. Pedro and the crew came by the house, and while they were setting up, I told Pedro all about Roger Clemens—how HarperCollins had pulled his name, and how *60 Minutes* had followed suit. "If you tell me this on air," he said, visibly excited, "I will lead *SportsCenter* with it."

I spent two hours with Gomez and told him everything. *On camera*. I told him what I knew and didn't know about

Clemens, and I told him about all of the other guys. It was a good interview, too, with all the requisite sound bites. I generally prefer television reporters to print, because the print guys tend to write exactly what they want, no matter what you tell them or how many times you tell them. But the TV guys can only work with what you give them. (Although a little selective editing can be pretty damaging.)

When ESPN aired Pedro's interview with me, Clemens's name was nowhere to be found. It wasn't the lead, and it wasn't in the body of the story.

What the hell was going on? Did the guy have connections that went beyond the White House? Was Clemens tight with the pope, too?

My agent called Pedro, who told him he had no idea why Clemens got cut from the piece. "I don't know what happened, Jose," my agent said. "It's a mystery."

"It sure is."

"I don't think Pedro knows why it was pulled, either."

"You can't believe anything these guys tell you! 'If you tell me about Clemens, I'll lead with it.' Sure, pal. Sure you will."

"I don't think it was him," my agent said.

"Nobody takes responsibility for anything anymore."

Man, it bugged me! Why was Clemens getting this free pass? What were all these people afraid of? Certainly not a baseless lawsuit! I had been told that Peter Angelos, owner of the Baltimore Orioles, had written a scathing letter to HarperCollins, threatening to sue everyone associated with the book, and their grandmothers, if they included Palmeiro's name in my book. In a previous incarnation,

Angelos had been a much-feared Baltimore litigator, but HarperCollins wasn't afraid of him or of the threatened lawsuit, and Palmeiro's name was left in the book, just as I had written it. So what scary guy was pulling strings for Roger Clemens? I wanted to know his name. I wanted it bad, even if it was just to know that I was tight with an eight-hundred-pound gorilla who would go to bat for me if I ever needed it. What this guy was doing for Roger was nothing short of miraculous. This guy was the guy behind the guy behind the guy behind the curtain. I wanted him on *my* team.

It was the weirdest thing. I understood that Clemens had weight; that he was an influential player; that he was widely respected; even that he was *important* to the game of baseball. But that didn't necessarily make him clean. That didn't necessarily mean he wasn't on steroids. That didn't mean the press couldn't let me talk about him.

And he wasn't *that* big. I had bigger names than Clemens, but I kept them out of the book for my own twisted reasons. And guess what? I'm going to share them with you now, and I'm going to make sure no one pulls them from this book. No, not this time. This time I'm going to give you more names. Big names. Two of the biggest names in baseball. One of them arguably *the* biggest name in baseball. Maybe the biggest name in the history of baseball.

But wait. I'm getting ahead of myself.

2

THE ENTERTAINERS

When someone gets around to writing the *real* history of baseball, I'm going to be remembered as the guy who did more to change the game than any other player. And I did it *twice*. I fundamentally changed the way the sport is played. The first time was when I introduced my fellow players to steroids, launching the Steroid Era, a decade that saw superhuman athletes breaking all of baseball's storied records. And the second time was when I saw that things were getting out of control, and that I had to tell the truth about what was going on.

Unfortunately, nobody wanted to hear the truth. I was excoriated by the press, booed by fans, and called a liar and a snitch by people who professed to care about the game. But here's the irony: nobody cared about the game as much as I did. And I have cared about it my whole life.

I was born in Cuba, and my parents moved to Florida

when me and my twin brother, Ozzie, were just kids. I liked baseball from early on, thanks to my father, who would take us out on weekends to teach us how to play. Or *try*, anyway. He seemed to enjoy telling us how terrible we were. But despite the insults, I refused to give up—maybe because I didn't want to be terrible, which I guess was his whole point.

We didn't have much money, but we did okay. And maybe that wasn't such a bad thing. As Joe DiMaggio once said, "A ballplayer's got to be kept hungry to become a big-leaguer. That's why no boy from a rich family ever made the big leagues."

When I was about eleven or twelve, I joined a local Little League, and my very first team was the Cincinnati Reds. I loved the uniform so much that I used to wear it to school under my regular clothes. The other kids made fun of me, but I didn't care. Baseball was already in my heart, my main interest in life.

In high school, I was kind of a runt—five-eleven, 165 pounds—but I was already seriously into baseball, and everything I did, every minute of every day, was designed to make me a better player. It was a struggle. I had pretty good hand-eye coordination, and I had a good swing, but things didn't quite click, and I didn't make the varsity team until senior year.

On Saturdays, I'd always watch *This Week in Baseball*, a television show. My favorite player was Reggie Jackson, but not because I aspired to be like him. He was such a god that to even fantasize about hitting like that seemed almost sinful. It was enough to just sit quietly, in awe, and watch.

In 1982, I was drafted by the Oakland Athletics, and I got off to a slow but steady start. Before long, however, I had really improved my swing, and on good days I was knocking 400-foot homers out of the park. The fans loved it. I noticed early on that fans reacted more to home runs than to anything else that happened on the field. As I began to hit more and more home runs, I became more of a crowd favorite. Every time I was up at bat, they'd cheer like crazy. They were looking to be entertained, and I was looking to be entertaining.

In 1984, my mother succumbed to a long illness. Toward the very end, I went home to say good-bye to her. I sat next to her, on her bed. She had slipped into a coma, but I took her hand in both of mine and promised her that someday I would become the best baseball player in the world. I'm sure she heard me. I imagined her smiling on the inside and saying, "I know you will, *hijo*. I never doubted you. I'll be watching from up there."

A week after the funeral, still in Miami, still grieving, I went off to the gym, to try to sweat out some of the pain. I ran into a friend of mine, a guy from high school, a weight lifter, and he could see I was an emotional wreck. We got to talking. I told him about my mother, and about the promise I'd made, and he could see I was determined to reach my goal. Well, as they say, one thing led to another, and before I knew it, he was injecting steroids into my gluteus maximus. And that's how it started. It was that simple.

I'm a kid in a gym, lost and weepy, and a friend offers me a way out. Or what I thought might be a way out.

Right after he shot me up, I half-expected to feel this huge rush, and that maybe I'd run into the street and flip cars over just for fun. After all, as a wrestler once put it, when you take steroids, you can just lie in bed and feel yourself grow. But that didn't happen. Nothing happened. I waited for that initial rush, and as I waited, I began to freak out a little. I wondered if I was going to develop a third eye, smack-dab in the middle of my forehead. Or if one of my arms was going to blow up like a balloon and pop. Or maybe I'd go home and look in the mirror and find a complete stranger staring back at me. None of that happened, of course. Nothing happened. At least at first. I finally noticed something about three weeks in, after taking steroids every day, and even then the change was gradual. One day, I was doing my regular workout, but it somehow felt much more efficient than what I was accustomed to. I felt like I had more energy, more of a pump. Within a month, I started gaining weight and seeing some real definition, and as the weeks went by, I felt myself getting stronger and stronger. I felt good about myself, too, confident, and that gave me a genuine psychological edge. I began to think, *Man, this stuff is really working!*

At that point, I honestly believed that steroids were going to help me keep my promise to my dying mother—nothing would stop me from getting better at baseball, nothing would stop me from being the best—and that's when the game really took over my life. It was the only thing that mattered. I didn't do drugs, and a beer or two was about all I could handle. And sure, I found women wonderfully distracting. But at the end of the day, it was all about baseball. That's all that mattered. I loved the game. I lived and breathed and dreamed the game.

And I kept at it, stayed focused on the goal. Everything I did was designed to make me a better player.

In 1986, I was named the American League's Rookie of the Year, and it began to look like I was on my way. But it wasn't happening by accident. After regular practice, while all the other players went off to the bars, I'd go to the gym and work out. On days off, I'd take more batting practice and hit the gym. I was going to turn myself into a baseball machine, for my mother, and I would do anything I had to do to get there. I read everything I could get my hands on about vitamins and supplements—even in bodybuilding magazines!—and I scoured other publications for new studies on steroids, growth hormones, and other performance-enhancing drugs.

The industry was still in its infancy back then, but I found that exciting, and I experimented with different products, becoming my own guinea pig. I tried every combination you can imagine. I was testing it on myself, and retesting, and mixing and matching every product on the market, trying things no one had ever imagined, and I was doing it to turn myself into a superathlete. I even kept notes! I had a journal where I would keep track of every detail, how much of this or that, when, how I felt twelve hours later, a *day* later, at the end of the *week*. I figured out how to eat to maximize the effectiveness of the steroids, how to train while taking them, and the best time of day to stick myself with the needle, during the season and in the off season. Before long, I was tipping the scales at 240 pounds, most of it muscle, so I was obviously doing something right.

The next year, 1987, Mark McGwire joined the Athletics, a tall, skinny kid with absolutely no muscle on him, and I guess he was impressed with my physique, because he had a lot of questions about my regimen.

The following year, not surprisingly, McGwire underwent a miraculous transformation, and shortly thereafter the fans began to call us the Bash Brothers. I wonder how that happened?

In 1988, I became the first player in major league history to hit 40 home runs (42, actually) and steal 40 bases in the same season. The 40-40 club had only one member, yours truly, and suddenly baseball fans were paying attention. It felt absolutely great. I had a .307 batting average, 120 runs scored, 124 runs batted in (the most in the league), and I also led the league in home runs, with my 42. As a result, I was named, unanimously, the American League's Most Valuable Player. And you know what? I was the first unanimously elected Most Valuable Player since Reggie Jackson, my hero.

When I was told about the award, it was an emotional moment for me. Only four years earlier I had promised my mother I'd become the best baseball player in the game. It was the last promise I made to her, and this Most Valuable Player award meant I had kept my promise. I was the best in the game. I had done something—the 40-40—that no other player had ever done before. The dedication, hard work, and focus had paid off, and in record time.

In 1989, however, I broke my wrist and missed half the season, but I still helped the Athletics win their first World Series in fifteen years (in the half I played, anyway). That, combined with my MVP title from the previous year, helped me land a five-year deal with Oakland for $23.5 million. At the time, it was the biggest contract ever for a baseball player.

The next year, my back started getting worse. I'd been having trouble with it since I was a kid, and suddenly I hit a wall. I was juicing up to get through it, which is not without some irony: that same year, steroids were finally added to the list of substances prohibited under baseball's drug policy. The Anabolic Steroid Control Act of 1990 reclassified them as Schedule III controlled substances, and the criminal penalties for their use were increased.

In 1992, late in the season, I got traded to the Texas Rangers. I wasn't happy, as Oakland had been my only home in baseball, but I tried to make the best of it, and the guys were welcoming. It was particularly good to be playing with Rafael Palmeiro, a fellow Cuban who grew up in Miami, on the same streets as me and my twin brother, Ozzie. I made friends with Pudge Rodriguez and Juan Gonzalez, Latinos like me. All three men made an effort to make me feel at home, and I returned the favor by lecturing them on the joys, and perils, of steroids. This was a drug, after all, and not without its dangers. Loss of hair, acne, shrinking testes—to name a few. I'd read about mood swings and surges of anger, too, and I'd had experiences with both of those myself, but they were part of my personality, and I can tell you unequivocally that they had nothing to do with steroids.

You couldn't blame all bad behavior, on and off the field, on steroids. Some people just behaved badly naturally, and who was to say it was 'roid rage? (I still remember the day Roger Clemens picked up a broken baseball bat in the middle of the 2000 World Series and chucked it at Mike Piazza as Mike ran to first base. What was *that* about?)

Before long, some of my new Rangers teammates were looking pretty buff and feeling good, and I warned them about getting too carried away. If you don't lay off the stuff from time to time, I told them, your body can lose its ability to produce its own testosterone. And you don't want to get *too* big. If those muscles got out of control, the tendons might not be able to support them. (That's what they say happened to Barry Bonds in 1999, when he blew out his elbow. But, really, what would I know? It's not like I have any real experience in this area, right? I mean, the man was clean, wasn't he?)

That same year, my debut year with the Rangers, we were playing against the Cleveland Indians and I was in the outfield. A long fly ball hit me in the head and bounced into the stands for a home run. It was pretty humiliating, and I'm sure you've seen that clip a bunch of times. (If you haven't, you can probably find it on YouTube.) The next year wasn't much better, and the year after that—1994— we had the baseball strike, which took the luster off a good year for me.

When we finally returned to the business of playing ball, I decided to claw my way back to respectability, and I got a little help from steroids. Or maybe *more* than a little. The juice made me stronger, faster, and better, and the fans noticed.

In 1998, I hit 46 home runs and stole 29 bases. It wasn't quite the 40 I'd stolen a decade earlier, but it felt good. If it had been a normal year, those numbers would've been all over the media, but nobody noticed because Mark McGwire and Sammy Sosa were in the middle of their home-run race, both of them determined to best Roger Maris's single-season record. The fans couldn't believe the way these guys were hitting—they'd never seen anything like it—but I was pretty sure I knew why. They were hitting the way they were hitting for the same reason I was hitting the way I was hitting: steroids. Baseball had been dying on the vine, but suddenly the game had a few rock stars, *buff* rock stars, and those rock stars were filling seats.

Did I say nobody noticed me? Well, allow me to correct myself. That same year, in September 1998, to be precise, a baseball writer described me as "the most conspicuous example of a player who has made himself great with steroids."

A day or two later, during a game against the Boston Red Sox in Toronto, if I'm remembering this correctly, some of the fans took it upon themselves to boo me when I stepped onto the field. I didn't let if faze me. Instead, I struck a pose—as my old friend Madonna might have done—and flexed my bulging muscles, Arnold Schwarzenegger–style. The crowd went nuts. It was showtime, folks. This was what sports in America were all about!

The following year I played for Tampa Bay, and I stayed with them for part of 2000. But I ended the year with the New York Yankees, who won the World Series. The next year, 2001, I was traded to the Chicago White Sox, and the year after that I signed with the Newark Bears, part of the independent Atlantic League. I then joined the Montreal Expos, which was the beginning of the end for me, and in May 2002, reluctantly, I retired from the game.

But that's not exactly the right way to put it. The fact is, I was pushed out. The owners had decided to make an example of me. By pushing me out, they gave everyone the impression that steroids would not be tolerated. Period. That wasn't the real message, though. Far from it. The real message was that they would be tolerated, even encouraged, just as long as the players were discreet. The real message was "Keep doing those steroids, and keep hitting those beautiful, 600-foot moon shots, but by God, don't get caught, boys. Because if you get caught, it's going to be tough to protect you." The owners were supposed to be trying to do something about the illegal use of steroids, or at least *look* as if they were trying, so they needed the players to be discreet and considerate. By blackballing me, the guy who had brought steroids into the game, Major League Baseball was telling its players not to get caught.

I'd had a respectable career—462 career home runs, four-time winner of the Silver Slugger Award, an MVP, World Series rings, and more fun than any man is legitimately entitled to—so it was hard to accept that it was really over. I was only 38 homers short of 500, and I was not going to be given a chance to reach that magic number. And I'll tell you, being kicked out like that hurt like hell.

I love baseball. No one knows how much I love this game. I played through three major back surgeries, a shoulder surgery, and several hand surgeries. I love the game for the electricity, for the fans, and for the chance to swing just right and launch that ball. There is nothing better than hitting a home run that travels five hundred, even six hundred feet. And I was good at it. When I went up to bat, the fans took note. "Here comes Jose. Prepare to be entertained." But now, suddenly, it was over. At the age of thirty-seven, I'd been turned into the poster boy for "plausible deniability." In getting rid of me, the bosses were not only acknowledging that baseball had a problem with steroids, but also alleged they were actually doing something about cleaning it up.

I remember going to a Dan Marino pro-am golf event shortly after I got dumped, and running into Alex Rodriguez. "You know what's going on, don't you?" he said.

"With what?"

"With the league. They're blackballing you."

"Yeah," I said. "I know."

It was hard to believe. Only four years earlier I had hit 46 home runs in a single season, something that maybe two or three dozen players had managed since baseball began, in the 1870s. Now I was expected to believe that there wasn't a single team in the entire league that could use a guy with my talent. In 2001, the last season I played, I batted .258 and hit 16 home runs in only 76 games. That's on pace for a 33-home-run season. Only eighteen guys in the entire league hit over 33 home runs in 2002!

The day after Alex Rodriguez stated the obvious, that I'd been blackballed, I ran into another player, Alex Fernandez, who told me the same thing. Not that I needed to be told. I had been out looking for another job, and not a single team would offer me a contract—not even at the league minimum. At one point, I offered to donate my salary to a local children's charity, but still nobody wanted me. They wouldn't take me for nothing. Hell, maybe they wouldn't have taken me if I'd offered to pay them.

I was so desperate to get back in the game, in fact, that I did an open tryout for the L.A. Dodgers, a team that was in miserable shape back then. I ran well, I threw well, and I hit well, but they still didn't want me. And man, it *burned*. I was 38 lousy home runs short of 500. That meant the world to me, but clearly it meant nothing to them.

I remember Tommy Lasorda telling me that the team didn't want me, and after I'd gone off, with my tail between my legs, he came running after me. "Jose!" he hollered.

I turned around. For a moment, my heart jumped. Maybe he'd just been messing with me, having a little fun. The team wanted me after all! "What?" I said tentatively, trying not to let my excitement get the better of me.

"You mind autographing this ball for me?"

Shit.

Later that week, I went to speak to Don Fehr, executive director of the Players Association, who said he'd try to help me. This is the guy who is in charge of taking care of players, making sure they are treated fairly, and I never heard from him again.

The whole experience was incredibly debilitating. I was just asking for a chance to show them I still had it, but they weren't interested. They took a piece of me, a piece of my heart, and it seemed to be the one piece that was holding me together.

Then, to add insult to injury, I ran into Barry Bonds. He and his wife were in L.A., having a house built, and I bumped into them when I was en route to pick up my daughter, Josie. The first words out of Barry's mouth, before even a hello, were straight to the point, but I didn't understand what the hell he was trying to tell me. "I'm not on steroids," he said. "I'm not doing anything." He picked up his shirt to show me his new, smaller body.

"Why are you telling me?" I said. "Why are you trying to make me believe that you're clean? Why would I give a shit?"

"What are you getting so upset about, man? I'm just *saying*."

As I drove off, I remembered an earlier meeting with Barry Bonds, and suddenly our little encounter made perfect sense. It was back in February 2000. We were in Las Vegas, for the Big League Challenge, a home-run-hitting contest at Cashman Field. I was given $100,000 just to show up, and I was told that the winner would take home $600,000. I'd just had back surgery, though, so I figured I'd be lucky to hit anything at all.

When we were in the locker room, changing before

going out onto the field, I took off my shirt and found Bonds staring at me, his eyes bugging out of his head. "Man," he said, "you are ripped!"

I guess I was. I looked like Dolph Lundgren in *Rocky IV*. There wasn't an ounce of fat on me (if I may say so myself). I was 255 pounds of chiseled, high-def power.

"You have to tell me what the hell you've being doing," he said.

"I'll tell you after the game," I said.

We went outside, and I knocked several moon shots out of the park, including twenty-eight bombs in the last round. I went home with the $600,000 enchilada.

Bonds hadn't even made the finals, and he was in a lousy mood, but he waited for me because he wanted us to have our little talk. I told him everything I knew. It was Jose Canseco's Guide to Steroids 101, and over the years I'd had that identical conversation with hundreds of other guys, players and nonplayers alike.

About a year later, when the regular season got under way, Bonds showed up with an extra thirty pounds on him, all of it muscle. And I'll be the first to tell you: you don't get that kind of muscle just from working out. It's literally impossible. Now, I'm not saying I saw him use the stuff, because I didn't, but I was pretty much an expert on the subject of steroids, and I can tell you that steroids had changed the man—including the size of his goddamn head. That head was hard to miss!

And of course his performance spoke volumes. Here was a guy who'd never broken 50 home runs in a single season, and suddenly he hits 73, breaking the previous major league record, McGwire's 70.

Even the fans couldn't believe the way he looked. "My God," they'd say. "Get a load of the size of him! The man is a monster."

And can you blame him? Bonds had watched McGwire take over the game, *his* game, and he was simply doing what he felt he had to do.

In retrospect, I'd have to say that this was when the press started paying a little attention to the problem. Some reporters had been trying, halfheartedly, to look into the story, but nobody wanted to hear it, and nobody was listening.

Rumblings about drug use in professional baseball went back to the late 1980s, when the Anti–Drug Abuse Act of 1988 was passed, creating criminal penalties for unauthorized use of anabolic steroids.

Nothing much happened, though. And nothing happened in 1995, when Randy Smith, the Padres general manager, sat down with a reporter from the *Los Angeles Times* and spelled it out for him. "We all know there's steroid use, and it's definitely becoming more prevalent," he said. Two players were also interviewed for the story, Tony Gwynn and Jason Giambi, and they were quick to back him up. They said that at least 30 percent of the guys on the field were using.

What they weren't telling them was this: steroids were a goddamn gift. They could take a mediocre player from the obscurity of the minor leagues to big money in the majors. For a more seasoned player, steroids led to new records—and maybe even the history books.

Mark McGwire was a perfect example of the benefits of steroids. He had always been a good hitter, but he began as a skinny kid with no muscle, and he bulked up until, in 1998, he broke Roger Maris's single-season home-run record. How'd he do it? Guess. Who cared? No one. Not even most of the reporters.

It's not as if they didn't notice, though. When reporters sat down to talk to me, I'd often catch them looking at my body, and I could see them thinking, *Are you even human?* That must've gone double for McGwire.

Then in August 1998, an Associated Press reporter found steroids in McGwire's locker. (Androstenedione, actually, a steroid-based dietary supplement.) This might not have been such a big deal, except that McGwire and Sosa were in the middle of chasing Roger Maris's 61-home-run record, so people paid attention.

McGwire had an answer for the press: "Everything I've done is natural. Everybody that I know in the game of baseball uses the same stuff I use."

That was almost enough to make the story go away, which is what Major League Baseball wanted. They even made excuses for McGwire. Andro was perfectly legal, they pointed out. It had been banned in the Olympics, sure, and the National Football League had banned it, too, but if it was really so terrible, how come you could walk into your local health-food store and find it on the shelves?

It wasn't until later, in 2002, at a hearing of the Senate

Commerce Committee, in Washington, D.C., that baseball commissioner Bud Selig, along with Don Fehr, executive director of the Major League Baseball Players Association (MLBPA), were told to make a strict drug-testing program part of the collective-bargaining negotiations for the new Basic Agreement.

This was not good news. MLB had been fighting for years to make sure the players *wouldn't* be tested for steroids. And it was easy to see why. They wanted players on the field that had superhuman powers. They wanted home runs. And they wanted steroid-enhanced athletes who were fun to watch. That's what put asses in the seats, and anything that stood in the way of that—anything that might be bad for the suddenly booming business of baseball—was just unacceptable. The Senate Commerce Committee must've been made up of a bunch of killjoys. Didn't they love baseball? Why couldn't they leave these nice, muscular boys alone?

Shit happens, though.

In August 2001, Korey Stringer, a lineman with the Minnesota Vikings, died in the middle of a summer workout, and the implication was that baseball wasn't the only sport with a little steroid problem. Nobody ever accused Stringer of juicing up, and nobody suggested he had, but people wondered, and that was enough. I'm sure it was hard on his family and friends.

Then in February 2003, Baltimore Orioles pitcher Steve Bechler collapsed and died during spring training. The cause was listed as heat exhaustion, but an autopsy found ephedra in his system, and the drug—a stimulant thought to enhance athletic performance—was immediately banned from the minor leagues.

Mandatory drug testing was put into place shortly thereafter, and during the 2003 season, the MLBPA announced that 5 to 7 percent of players had tested positive.

In September of that same year, federal agents raided the offices of the Bay Area Laboratory Co-Operative (BALCO), operated by Victor Conte. A number of world-class athletes were allegedly getting performance-enhancing drugs from the organization, and ten major league players were subsequently called to testify in front of a San Francisco grand jury. These included Barry Bonds, who was with the Giants, and Jason Giambi and Gary Sheffield, of the Yankees. (Dozens of professional football players were also implicated, along with track star Marion Jones, but that's another story.) None of the baseball players were actually charged with using performance-enhancing drugs, but Bonds's personal trainer, Greg Anderson, was indicted for money laundering and for selling steroids without prescriptions.

Later, the plot thickened. A pair of reporters at the *San Francisco Chronicle,* who later went on to write the book *Game of Shadows,* found out that some of the players had been notified before their so-called random tests. And the following year, the same reporters got hold of transcripts from the grand jury hearings and published some choice sections. Giambi, for example, flat out admitted that he had injected himself, and Bonds said he might have taken steroids, unwittingly, when his personal trainer rubbed a cream on his legs that possibly contained the illegal substance.

What the hell did people expect? If you wanted to compete, you needed steroids. You couldn't naturally gain thirty pounds of muscle in three months, and the competition was gaining that and more. If you didn't do steroids, you lost your edge.

What were people not seeing? Steroids had changed the game. They were changing the way the game was played. They were changing the record books.

And here's the thing: everyone knew. Nothing happened in the clubhouse that wasn't approved by the ownership. From top to bottom, the whole thing was institutionalized. Everybody knew about the bogus B_{12} shots, and everyone was using them. And you want to know why they were using them? They were using them because they were afraid of losing their jobs. It's that simple. They had to perform to stay in the game, and steroids gave them the edge they needed. I know this because I loved that edge and I came to need it, and it got to a point where I knew I'd be lost without it.

Think about it in terms of your own life. If somebody said, "Here. Take this painless little shot. It'll make you better at your job, and your financial future will be all but secured." What would you do? I know what I would do. Hell, I know what I *did*.

Even the sports agents were in on it. The more money a client made, the more the agent made. Agents wanted their players to be big and strong and fast, so that they could compete well and get increasingly lucrative contracts.

And it's funny, because there was actually a story in a paper back then, I believe it was the *Atlanta Journal-Constitution,* in which someone took a player's height, weight, and body mass, and, using a bizarre semiscientific formula, was able to determine what kind of salary he might expect. The conclusion? Over an eight-year period, the salaries of the jumbo-size players increased by about 60 percent over those of their medium-size counterparts. Is there a moral to the story? Yeah, I guess: steroids make you rich. Big and rich.

The same thing was going on in wrestling. In track. In cycling. In the Olympics. It became an international phenomenon. At one point, I heard they were thinking of testing *golfers*!

What can I tell you? Steroids had taken over sports.

3

THE FOGGY MIRROR

In 2002, *Sports Illustrated* did a story about Ken Caminiti, a three-time Gold Glove winner, who admitted he had used steroids during his 1996 season, when he was named MVP, and for several seasons afterward. Up until that point, no professional baseball player had ever made such a public admission, and Caminiti's announcement had a huge effect on other players, mostly because—like all self-absorbed athletes—they were worried about being exposed. Reporters were affected, too, but mostly because they hadn't bothered to investigate a story that had been staring them in the face for almost two decades.

In the article, Caminiti said that at least half of the players in the major leagues were using steroids, a figure that was probably hard to determine, but certainly not hard to believe (not for me, anyway). It was right around that time that I first began to think about writing a book on the whole Steroid Era. Caminiti's revelations made me think about some of my experiences over the years, on and off the field, and about many of the guys I knew. I wanted to write an honest book about the game, and about some of the problems that were changing it, and I soon realized that I wouldn't be able to do it without naming names. If I wanted to tell the truth, the whole, unvarnished truth, if I wanted to pull back the curtain on this conspiracy of silence, I would have to dive in with my eyes open. Even if it pissed people off.

I thought about some of the guys I'd want to include in the book. Mark McGwire was a must. He was the most prolific right-handed power-hitter in the game, and he and Sammy Sosa basically "saved baseball," as every sports reporter in the country kept telling us. We all knew how they did it, of course, but McGwire was still a mystery to me in other ways: he left the game when he was within view of 600 career home runs, with a $27 million contract being dangled as bait. What the hell was that all about? Was he worried? Did he think he was about to be found out?

Jason Giambi was another player I'd have to include in the book. Some MLB execs talked him into admitting that he used steroids and, as soon as he did, handed him a multimillion-dollar contract. (Way to stop the scourge of drugs, guys! Way to put more of a premium on a player's entertainment value than on his health! Way to use steroids to sell the game!)

Then there was Sammy Sosa, another skinny kid who bulked up.

In October 2004, while I was putting the finishing

touches on my book, Caminiti died, felled by a heart attack that was traced to two drug overdoses. That summer, as a direct result of the tragedy, Major League Baseball was pressured to get tougher by including steroid testing in its new labor agreement.

On the heels of Caminiti's death, some players decided to get honest, or *semi*honest. A number of them hung their heads in mock shame and said they'd used steroids once or twice, maybe even by accident. Right! The poor bastard accidentally sat on a needle, and it accidentally went right into his butt cheek, which he wasn't aiming for. There is no such thing as a onetime user, people, and all the guys knew that. To heal, and to build genuine muscle, you've got to commit to a six-week cycle, minimum. Those chemicals need to build inside your system, and that takes time. Nobody uses it just once.

There were also plenty of stories about steroid cream, which guys apparently kept slathering on by accident. Or it kept getting slathered on by their trainers when they weren't looking. "I never *knowingly* took steroids or other performance-enhancing drugs!"

Jesus, how naive are we? If you're a professional athlete, one of the elite, you know exactly what you're eating, how hard you're working out, how much you're sleeping, what (legal) supplements you're taking, and what (illegal) substances you're injecting. Your body is your career, and you watch anything and everything connected to it.

You had no idea what your trainer was doing! Of course! That makes total sense. But when you're at Starbucks, you watch the kid behind the counter like a hawk—

"Are you sure that was nonfat milk? That didn't look like nonfat milk. Nonfat milk doesn't foam like that"—but your trainer comes at you with a needle, and *that* you don't notice. Please. Spare us the nonsense.

The more I thought about the story, the more I felt it needed to be told. Plus I had the research at my fingertips. Every time I was mentioned in the paper, or in a magazine, and every time anything popped up on the steroid scandal, I'd read it carefully—I guess I had too much time on my hands—and add it to the growing pile of articles in my house. I suppose in that sense I took after my dad: he collected videos of every single one of the 462 home runs I hit in my career, then put them on a DVD. The man could sit there for hours, watching me hit, which was a good feeling, mostly because he hadn't seemed too interested in me, or too impressed, when I was a kid.

So I made a few calls and went to a few meetings, and before long I got a deal to write my book. I hired a ghostwriter because I knew I'd need help shaping my many thoughts into a compelling true story, and we were off and running.

And here's the thing: I had been thinking about this story for so long, whether consciously or not, that the words just poured out of me. And I'll tell you something else: it felt good. It felt like I was doing something important, like I was telling a story that was way bigger than anything I had first imagined. As I told my story, I kept thinking, *Man, this is a good story. I'm glad I'm finally sharing it with the world.*

Within a few months, there was a knock at the door. It

was UPS with a delivery from HarperCollins: the galleys of my book. I couldn't believe it. The book was almost done. But standing there, holding an advance copy, made it suddenly real.

Then, at the beginning of February 2005, when we were just a couple of weeks from publication, the *Miami Herald* leaked portions of the book, and as I said earlier, the shit hit the fan.

The publisher did a little damage control. We moved up the date of publication, moved up the interview with *60 Minutes*, and had the book in stores by mid-February.

More shit hit the fan, and it never stopped.

Curt Schilling: "I think he's a liar. I think what he did was grossly overstate a situation to make himself not look as bad."

Kevin Blackistone of the *Dallas Morning News:* "I thought the guy was lying through his teeth. He had said at one point that he didn't do steroids. And here he was saying now, 'I did do steroids, and so did everybody else.' "

Rick Reilly, of *Sports Illustrated* and ESPN: "Baseball, more than any sport, is full of lies, and liars, and cheaters."

David Letterman and Jay Leno were making jokes about me—don't worry, I could handle it—and Jimmy Kimmel was performing skits. And it was all pretty much on message: *Canseco is nuts. Canseco doesn't know what he's talking about. Canseco is broke and did the book because he needed the money. Canseco is a big, fat liar.*

While all the criticism started to weigh on me personally, when it came to book sales, it only helped. The book shot to the top of the *New York Times* bestseller list, and it stayed there. Meanwhile, of course, people kept calling me a liar and a sore loser and other things I won't deign to print in this family-friendly book.

I handled it, though. Despite the one week I spent in near-total isolation, I emerged from my lair and faced the press and did hundreds of interviews.

And by the way, when I finally went on the *Today* show, Matt Lauer and his team turned out to be as unpleasant as the woman who'd done the pre-interview. For starters, they wouldn't let my lawyer, Rob Saunooke, join me on camera.

"We don't do that," they told us. "It's network policy."

"Network policy?" Rob replied politely. "Every time I turn on the *Today* show, there's someone sitting on the couch with his lawyer next to him."

"Well, it's just not going to work this time."

Rob looked over at me and told me not to worry about it. "Just get out there and do your thing and we'll move on."

So I went off to face Matt Lauer, who was a complete asshole—to put it quite bluntly. He was incredibly aggressive, very much in my face, and he seldom let me finish answering a question. I'd begin to say something that I thought was clearly cogent and believable, and he'd cut me off and move on to the next topic. Attack, attack, attack. Like a lot of reporters, he didn't believe me and didn't want to hear my story. *The stories I was telling couldn't possibly be true.*

I'll tell you, if my temper wasn't always under my full

control, I could have gotten very pissed off, but I sucked it up and tried to make the best of an unpleasant situation. I survived, but on my way out—believe it or not—Lauer actually asked me to autograph a copy of *Juiced* for him. The gall!

I was still steamed, of course, maybe more steamed, but I didn't let my feelings show until I was far from the set. "Jesus, that Lauer—what a jerk!" I said.

"Completely inappropriate," Rob said, agreeing with me.

"What have I ever done to him?"

"It's not him, Jose. It's baseball. People don't want to believe what you have to say."

"I knew that going in, but I didn't think telling the truth was going to be this difficult."

"Just keep doing what you're doing. They'll get the message. Eventually."

"I don't want to wait for eventually," I said. "Eventually could be a very long way off. I'm dealing with this right now, every day."

I kept plugging along, though, waiting for the tide to turn. And I handled it. Mostly because I didn't have a choice. I handled everything and everyone, reporters large and small. The one or two who believed me, and the hundreds—maybe thousands—who didn't want to and probably never would.

And that's what hurt the most. That people refused to accept that I was telling the whole, unvarnished truth. *Liar liar liar!* That was the refrain, and it stayed with me. I had written an honest book, for *mostly* honorable reasons, and they couldn't see it. It was unbelievably frustrating. I had written the truth but people still insisted on calling me a liar. I guess they only saw what they wanted to see, and what they wanted to see was that I couldn't possibly be telling the truth about the hallowed game of baseball. As far as they were concerned, I had written the book solely to punish the owners who had tossed me out, and to expose some of the game's less-than-honest players.

I stayed tough, though. I had to stay tough. I knew the truth would come out. *Eventually*. Or at least I told myself that to keep trudging along, to keep smiling.

In the middle of the book tour, while I was running around the country greeting fans, I got a death threat. My attorney was smart enough to take it seriously, and he contacted the FBI.

As it turned out, some misguided nineteen-year-old kid from Arkansas felt I had shattered his dreams. He had all sorts of illusions about the Sacred Game of Baseball, illusions that were likely shared by most of the rest of the country, and he hated me for all the terrible things I'd said about the game. I guess he preferred to live in the dark, ignoring what was obviously happening on the field.

I had illusions, too—specifically that the book tour would go on—but I was wrong. I was told that the book tour was over, and I was sent home.

After all the hoopla, things died down abruptly, and the phone pretty much stopped ringing. I didn't hear from a single player—not an iota of support—and even some of the people I'd considered friends stopped calling. Not that it bothered me, though. Not much, anyway. I'm not the party guy people think I am. I'm really just a homebody, and I believe that healthy doses of isolation are good for the soul.

A few weeks later, with the press still taking nasty shots at me, somebody reported a story about an FBI investigation into the world of steroids. "There's very little question the use of steroids was very widespread in baseball and Major League Baseball," according to FBI special agent Greg Stejskal, who worked out of the Ann Arbor, Michigan, office and was part of the investigation, known as Operation Equine. "In effect, they didn't sanction it, but they certainly looked the other way."

The FBI had been focused on busting steroid dealers, but they thought the findings were so significant that they wasted no time in reporting them to Major League Baseball, specifically to MLB security chief Kevin Hallinan. Nothing happened, and Hallinan never bothered to follow up with the FBI.

Later, when the busts were made, and the dealers were carted off, the press began to pay attention. But MLB acted as if this had nothing to do with baseball.

Still, as some of the details began to emerge, a few people actually started wondering if maybe, just maybe, I'd been telling the truth. Not enough to make a difference, mind you, but a few. And it felt as if the pendulum was starting to swing my way.

It wasn't only baseball, by the way. The Feds were looking for dealers, and the clues had led directly to the dark heart of baseball, but other professional sports were also implicated, and there was even talk of involvement by Olympic athletes.

The part that got to me, however, was this business about the powers-that-be in Major League Baseball, how they chose to ignore the problem. But it didn't surprise me: the baseball bosses doing nothing was about par for the course. Or maybe it surprised me a little: that they could still do nothing after being tipped by the Feds, that was hard to believe. Then, as if that weren't enough, MLB denied that they had ever had the meeting with Special Agent Stejskal. That's what they were good at, denial, and they just kept denying it. (And they kept denying it until 2008!)

In March 2005, a month after the publication of my book, Congress launched its investigation into the steroid scandal, and MLB officials were told that they needed to beef up their drug program immediately. If they didn't, according to Representative Henry Waxman, Congress would do it for them, "and you don't want that."

I was asked to appear before Congress, and my attorney, Rob, met me in Miami to help me prepare. I didn't want to go, but my reasons had nothing to do with baseball. I had no problem sharing everything I knew with Congress, but I was worried that something I said might get me tossed back into a Florida jail.

I talked about my stint behind bars in my previous book, so I'll keep it short. In 2004, I was in California to see my daughter and to play in a charity golf tournament. At the time, I was on probation in Florida, as a result of a long-ago bar fight, and I got back to Miami a day late. I was immediately arrested, sentenced to thirty days behind bars, and upon my release was placed under house arrest for two years.

Several months later, my twin brother, Ozzie, was found driving with a suspended license. When the police searched his car, they found a bottle of steroids and a needle. This happened some three hundred miles from where I was living, serving out my house arrest, but the police decided that I was somehow connected, and I was immediately picked up and tested for steroids.

It had been over a year since I'd done any steroids, but a minuscule amount—no more than remnants, really—were found in my system. I was nailed on a steroids charge and locked in a tiny cell, and this turned into the most harrowing period of my entire life. You want a small taste of it? All the jumpsuits were ripped at the seams to make it easier to rape guys. I didn't have to worry about that, of course, because I'm pretty big, and because I can take care of myself, but that was my life, day in, day out—I was surrounded by animals.

For the next three months, as I rotted in prison, two men in the state attorney's office did everything in their power to keep me behind bars. I think they were basically using my name, and my case, to further their careers, and I was only released after their boss intervened. But I knew that those two were still looking to nail me, even after all this time, and I was genuinely worried. "I'm not going to testify," I kept telling Rob. "Those assholes in Miami are looking for anything that might lock me up for life."

"Jose, let's concentrate on one thing at a time," Rob said. "Stop worrying."

He had been working with Congressman Tom Davis, one of the guys running the hearings, to try to get me some level of immunity, so that I could answer questions without fear of reprisal, but it wasn't happening. "I can't stop worrying," I said. "The thought of going back to jail is making me sick to my stomach."

"You're not going to go to jail," Rob said.

"Are you sure?"

"Of course I'm not sure," Rob said. "But if we cooperate with Congress, maybe we will find some support there."

Somehow, Rob made me believe that my testimony could actually help my situation, so—even without immunity—we flew to D.C. for the hearings.

The night before the hearings, Rob and I had dinner with Congressman Davis and a few members of his staff. We again raised the question of immunity, and were told, again, that it wasn't going to happen. At that point, I definitely didn't want to testify, but Rob talked me down and assured me it was the right thing to do.

The following morning, as Rob and I were en route to the Ways and Means building, in a limousine provided by Congressman Davis, Rob's cell phone rang. It was Congressman Davis. He told Rob that Mark McGwire's attorneys were also trying to get immunity, but that it wasn't likely to happen. If it did, however, he would make sure that I got immunity, too.

"Okay," Rob told Congressman Davis. "We're on our

way over now, but do what you can. We'll take anything you've got, even limited immunity." He ended the call and turned to look at me and shook his head: "Not going to happen."

I was sick with worry. The guys in the district attorney's office in Miami really had it in for me. They would do anything to nail me. I was still on probation. If I said the wrong thing in that room that day, it could come back to haunt me for the rest of my life.

"There's nothing we can do about it now," Rob said. "You're as ready as you're going to be. Read the statement we've prepared and we'll see what happens, and if things get dicey, I'll be right behind you."

When the limo dropped us off, Rob and I were taken to a room in the bowels of the building. We were alone in there, far from the other players, and it only confirmed the feeling that it was truly us against them.

We waited for hours—or it *felt* like hours, anyway. When we were finally brought into the hearing room, I saw that all the other players were already there. The place fell deathly silent as we made our way inside. It was unbelievable. I was overwhelmed by the size of the room, and the amount of people in it—congresspeople, reporters, lawyers. And all of them were staring at us. I remember thinking, *It really is me and Rob against the rest of the world.* Against MLB. Against the players. Against the Players Association. Against the press. Against everyone. Just a couple of Davids against an army of Goliaths. I was nervous, I'll admit it. *Beyond* nervous, actually, but we were past the point of no return. We moved to our places and I waited, trying to remember to breathe. When it was my turn to speak, I turned to the pages in front of me and plunged in:

Mr. Chairman, members of the Committee, distinguished guests; I am humbled by this opportunity to appear before you today. Never in my wildest dreams could I have imagined that my athletic ability and love for America's game would lead me to this place and the subject that has brought me before the Committee. When I decided to write my life's story, I was aware that what I revealed about myself and the game I played for a majority of my life would create a stir in the athletic world. I did not know that my revelations would reverberate in the halls of this chamber and in the hearts of so many.

I had hoped that what I experienced firsthand, when revealed, would give insight into a darker side of a game that I loved. That maybe it would force baseball to acknowledge [that] it condoned this activity for the sole purpose of increasing revenue at the gate. Unfortunately, by our presence here today, it is clear that MLB is not interested in admitting the truth. It is also clear that although others have tried to come out in support of my revelations, fear of repercussions from MLB haunts their conscience.

The book that I wrote was meant to convey one message. The preface makes my position very clear. I do not condone or encourage the use of any particular drugs, medicine, or illegal substances in any aspect of life. My book was informational and intended to enlighten the world about a problem that until my book was released had only been spoken of in whispers. I did not write my book to single out any one individual or player. I am saddened that the media and others have chosen to focus on the names in the book and not on the real culprit behind the issue. That the focus of my life and those involved in it may have inadvertently damaged players was not my intent. I hoped rather that finally the media and the world would try and dig beyond the easy answer and not fix blame but fix the problem. A problem that would continue unabated if I did not call attention to it.

Because of my truthful revelations, I have had to endure attacks on my credibility. I have had to relive parts of my life that I thought had been long since buried and gone. All of these attacks have been spurred on by an organization that holds itself above the law. An organization that chose to exploit its players for the increased revenue that lines its pockets and then sacrifice those same players to protect the web of secrecy that was hidden for so many years. The time has come to end this secrecy and to confront those who refuse to acknowledge their role in encouraging the behavior we are gathered to discuss.

I love the sport of baseball. I love it in its purest and simplest form. I still long for the time when I could pick up a bat and ball and hit one over the fence for the game-winning run. I am appreciative of the opportunities that the sport of baseball has given to me along with the quality of life it has provided. It permitted me to take care of my family and provide a better life for myself and others close to me. However, had I known that this opportunity would cost me so much, I would have refused the offer so many years ago.

The pressure associated with winning games, pleasing fans, and getting the big contract, led me, and others, to engage in behavior that would produce immediate results. This is the same pressure that leads the youth of today, other athletes and professionals, to engage in that same behavior. The time has come to address this issue and set the record straight about what risks are involved in that behavior. To send a message to America, especially the youth, that these actions, while attractive at first, may tarnish and harm you later. That sometimes there are things more important than simply money.

Why did I take steroids? The answer is simple. Because myself and others had no choice if we wanted to continue playing. Because MLB did nothing to take it out of the sport. As a result, no one truly knew who was on muscle-enhancing drugs. As a result, a player who wanted to continue to play, to perform as a star, was forced to put into their bodies whatever they could just to compete at the same level as those around them.

However, why we are before Congress today is only part of a much larger problem. The American public continues to place athletes in a position above everyone else. "Some people are born to greatness and others have greatness thrust upon them." A successful athlete is viewed as the voice of a city, state, and country. He or she, in playing their sport, often represents the very spirit of a nation and its people. We rarely see riots and the gut-wrenching emotion so apparent in sports in any other forum. When the Boston Red Sox failed to get to the World Series two years ago, the pain echoed throughout the fans as a personal attack on the city and on the individual residents there. When a Chicago Cubs fan got caught up in the moment and interfered with the game, he was attacked, vilified, and forced to move and change his life.

Such emotional investment is felt by the players daily. We want only to please those who hold us in such high esteem. We feel deeply the obligation that we each have to perform and win. It is a burden that we take on willingly and without hesitation or regret. However, perhaps in addition to addressing this pressing issue we should take the opportunity to look at the priority that we place on athletes and athletics and change our focus.

Baseball owners and the players' union have been very much aware of the undeniable fact that as a nation we will do anything to win. They turned a blind eye to the clear evidence of steroid use in baseball. Why? Because it sold tickets and resurrected a game that had recently suffered a black eye from a player strike. The result was an intentional act by baseball to promote, condone, and encourage the players to do whatever they had to do to win games, bring back the fans, and answer the bottom line. Salaries went up, revenue increased, and owners got richer. But this comes with a cost.

MLB issued press releases years ago stating clearly the position that banned substances that enhanced performance were not a part of MLB. MLB set forth "for cause testing" to support this position. However, during my entire career no player was ever tested for performance-enhancing substances. "For cause" became a hollow threat that was never used by anyone involved with MLB. It was again made clear that press releases were the only thing MLB was going to do to "clean up" MLB's image. The duplicity present throughout my career continues today.

Many have said that my motivation for revealing this problem is myriad: revenge, monetary gain, vindication. The truth is that I would have played baseball for free. I even offered to play for free some years ago and to donate my salary to charity just to be a part of the game. This offer was rejected and MLB turned its back on me just as it had turned a blind eye to the drugs that were running rampant through the sport. My motivation is nothing more than a clearing of conscience and an effort to resurrect a sport that has given joy to so many.

I am moved by the efforts Congress is taking to

address this problem. I am humbled that my book may have played a small part in setting forth this juggernaut. I am hopeful that it will yield a positive result.

As I sit here today, I would be remiss if I did not again stress that I do not condone the use of any drugs or illegal substances. I urge parents to become more active and involved in the lives of their children. I hope that my message will be received as it is intended, that we, as professional athletes, are no better than anyone else. We just have a special ability that permits us to play ball. We should not be held up to any higher standard of behavior than any other mother or father. Our children's heroes should not be solely the athletes they watch, but more important, the parents who are with them each day.

Thank you for this opportunity to appear before you. I hope that my statements and answers to those questions posed to me will help find a solution to this problem. That the intentional failure of MLB to address this issue will finally be put to rest, and that those who follow me into this sport will have the opportunity to do so free of the pressure to compromise themselves simply for increased revenue.

To those players who have been thrust into this debate I simply ask them to tell the truth as I have told the truth. To join with me and help resurrect the sport we love from where the owners and union have let it go.

Thank you.

When I was finished, the other guys launched in, and one by one they attacked me. I knew every word I had written was true, that I had been honest to a fault, and these guys sat in front of Congress and had the audacity to lie to Congress. It was insane. Mark McGwire, who looked to be close to tears half the time, said he wouldn't dignify my book with a response, then tried to put his own spin on matters: "I'm not here to discuss the past. I'm here to be positive about this." Before long, however, he was taking the Fifth: "My lawyers have advised me that I cannot answer these questions without jeopardizing my friends, my family, or myself. I intend to follow their advice."

I thought that was a huge mistake. In my opinion, anyone who takes the Fifth is already guilty. And I guess, for once, the sports media agreed with me. For the next few days, everyone's favorite line was "I'm not here to talk about the past." And it was always delivered with a smirk.

Rafael Palmeiro did something even stranger. He wagged his finger and flat out denied that he'd ever done anything illegal. Prior to his appearance before the committee, he had submitted to Congress sworn testimony as follows: "Let me start by telling you this: I have never used steroids, period. I do not know how to say it any more clearly than that. The reference to me in Canseco's book is absolutely false."

Wow! Rafael and I had been with the Texas Rangers at the same time, along with Juan Gonzalez and Ivan Rodriguez, right after I got traded by Oakland, and I'm here to tell you, I injected each of those three guys myself, with HGH, and with Deca.

Curt Schilling also testified, but I couldn't make much sense of what he said. He was supposed to be on some kind of committee against steroids, but the guy seemed to be on another planet. Over the years, he had told reporters that he knew plenty of players who shot up, and he said stuff to the effect that the worst offenders got so big that even their heads blew up, which made them look a little like the Pillsbury Doughboy. But a few weeks later he was telling another newspaper that he didn't think baseball had a problem with steroids, and he said he didn't know what the hell all the fuss was about. He was equally confused during his testimony, and he was repeatedly reprimanded.

As for Sammy Sosa, he conveniently forgot how to speak English—during the hearing, anyway—so he had his lawyer speak for him. And what the lawyer said on Sosa's behalf was fairly predictable: Sammy had never done any illegal drugs in his life, not in the United States and not in his native Dominican Republic.

It was surreal. Every time one of these guys denied having taken steroids, he was calling me a liar. And that burned. It was almost as if the charges had a cumulative effect on me: *Liar liar liar!* Is that what people were going to be calling me for the rest of my life? Was there going to be a picture of me in the dictionary, next to the word *liar*?

Liar. n. a person who has lied or who lies repeatedly. (syn: prevaricator). Talk to Jose Canseco. He knows better than anyone—better even than Pinocchio.

At one point, with all these guys skating around the questions, one of the congresspeople looked close to despair: "It seems as if Jose Canseco is the only player in this room who ever used steroids."

That's how crazy it was. And the craziest part, for me, was Rafi Palmeiro. I couldn't stop thinking about his testimony, and about the way he'd delivered it—with such vehemence and such assurance. The thing is, when Palmeiro lied like that, it suddenly hit me that the story was even bigger than I'd imagined. I had heard a rumor, unsubstantiated, that Palmeiro had *already* been tested, and that he'd tested positive. And I'd been told—also just a rumor—that MLB was trying to make a deal with him. And the funny thing is, the more I thought about it, the more sense it made. The bastards were doing everything in their power to discredit me. Even having a player lie under oath directly to the U.S. Congress.

I could almost see what had happened. These guys went to Palmeiro: "Hey, Rafi, we've got bad news and good news. The bad news is, you tested positive for steroids, and if it gets out, you're finished. The good news is, if you get up in front of Congress, and you wag your finger, and you emphatically deny ever having done steroids, we'll back you a hundred percent."

And in my fevered imagination, Palmeiro might have asked, "And why would you do that for me?"

"Because baseball needs your help. We want to discredit Canseco. We need everyone to believe that everything he has said about steroids in baseball is a lie, and we want the world to know it. If you go up to Congress, stare right at them, and at the television-viewing audience, and do your best to convince them that Canseco is lying, we will bend over backward to help you."

Now, you may take that for paranoid rambling, but it was *my* rambling, and I believed it. I knew something shady was up. I knew Major League Baseball would go to great lengths to discredit me and to ruin my reputation. I had too many years of experience watching Major League Baseball pull shady moves, lying to get what they wanted, colluding to make more money for themselves no matter whom they hurt, no matter what the law said.

By the time we took a break from the hearings, I was livid. Every player in that hearing had attacked me, and I hadn't been given an opportunity to defend myself. It seemed that they could say whatever they wanted about me with impunity.

At that point, the committee decided to take a brief adjournment. The moment we stepped outside, I told Rob that I wasn't going back. He got hold of Congressman Davis and really let him have it. "We were led to believe that we were coming here today to answer some general questions, not to be attacked in that manner," Rob said. "Every single one of those guys went on the offensive! Schilling. Palmeiro. McGwire. Sosa. We came here to cooperate and you said you'd protect us, but you're not protecting us. You're letting these guys attack the one honest person in that room, and not a single one of your congressmen came to Jose's defense. We're leaving!"

Davis said we couldn't leave, that we were under subpoena, but Rob didn't care—he was as mad as I was, maybe madder. "Subpoena or not, we're not going back inside without a guarantee that this is going to stop," he said. "I'm not subjecting my client to further attacks."

"Look," Davis said, "I'll take care of it. I promise. We were also misled. Baseball told us they were going to come in and cooperate, and they didn't, so we're dealing with that, too. It will be much different when we get back from the break."

We didn't know it at the time, but both Davis and Representative Henry Waxman had been negotiating with baseball to find a way to calm the waters. They had expected those buffoons to show up, to admit there was a problem, and to promise to start working to take care of it, but Major League Baseball didn't send anyone. Baseball once again tried to pull a fast one.

"I assure you," Davis said, "if you come back into the room, I guarantee that everything will change. We aren't letting them off that easy."

As it turned out, Davis kept his word. Following the break, the congressmen began by attacking Schilling's credibility, and they eventually got around to asking me direct questions. One of the first ones was about the guys who ran Major League Baseball, and why, in my opinion, they had done nothing about the growing scandal. "I guess in baseball, at the time, there was a saying, 'If it's not broke, don't fix it,'" I said. "And baseball was coming back to life. Steroids were part of the game. And I don't think anyone really wanted to take a stance on it."

When I was asked if I thought the owners and the coaches were aware of the problem, I said they were most definitely aware of it, and I even had a suggestion for how they might begin to handle the issue: "I think, in my opinion, the most effective thing right now would be for us to admit there is a major problem. It's got to start here. And we've got to admit certain things we've done, and change things there. From what I'm hearing, more or less, I was the only individual in Major League Baseball who used steroids. So, that's hard to believe."

I went on—I'd been given a platform, and I used it: "If Congress does nothing about this issue, it will go on forever . . . [and] trickle down to the minor league level, the high school level, and beyond."

And I kept hammering away at them: "I'm going to say this again: if Congress does nothing about this, Major League Baseball will not regulate themselves. The Players Association will not regulate these players. That, I guarantee."

The hearing had some pretty tough moments, but they had nothing to do with my testimony. They occurred when examples of how steroids can negatively affect lives were discussed. At one point, for example, Representative Waxman took time to acknowledge the family of Efrain Marrero, a nineteen-year-old football player from California who killed himself while he was on steroids. It was an emotional moment for me, and probably everyone in the room and everyone watching on television. And he wasn't the only victim. Another young man, Taylor Hooten, a high school baseball player, also committed suicide after using anabolic steroids, and the panel heard from his father, Don: "I believe the poor example being set by professional athletes is a major catalyst fueling the high usage of steroids amongst our kids. Our kids look up to these guys. They want to do the things the pros do to be successful. . . . Our youngsters hear the message loud and clear, and it's wrong. 'If you would want to achieve your goal, it's okay to use steroids to get you there, because the pros are doing it.' It's a real challenge for parents to overpower the strong message that's being sent to our children by your behavior."

He was right. Kids like Taylor looked up to us—to some of the guys in that very room—and we were flaunting our bad behavior. They all sat there knowing exactly what they had done and lied and deceived to hide their past. And what was the punishment? Multimillion-dollar contracts. Praise. Accolades.

There was only one point in the hearing when I thought that perhaps things might actually change, and that was toward the end of the day, when Congressman Dutch Ruppersberger suggested that one day everyone would be thanking me for single-handedly trying to save baseball. He was the only person in that room to publicly thank me for helping to spur the crackdown on doping in baseball.

After the hearing, Rob and I were just exhausted, but we decided that instead of sitting around a hotel room we'd go to dinner. We went over to Smith & Wollensky. Even though we didn't have a reservation, and the place was ridiculously crowded, the girl at the front desk seemed happy to see us and immediately escorted us to a choice table. Before we'd even settled in, several fans had stopped by to get my autograph, or to ask if they could take a picture with me, and I was happy to accommodate every last one of them. And everyone who approached me was incredibly supportive. They went out of their way to tell me how much they appreciated what I was doing to clean up the game of baseball, and their kind words gave me a real emotional boost. I knew I had been doing a good thing, despite what the press, the other players, and Major League Baseball had been trying to say, and it was nice to hear it from the fans—the people who really counted. I actually felt good.

"What a weird day," I said.

"Yeah," Rob said. "We go in there, believing that baseball wants to take your allegations seriously, and the sons of bitches pounce. At least things got a little better when we went in after the break. I loved the way they went after Schilling."

"You think anything's going to come of it?" I asked.

"Who knows? I hope so. I don't think Major League Baseball can just bury this one."

"I hope you're right."

"And that McGwire," Rob went on. "Can you imagine?"

"Imagine what?"

"While he was testifying, all I could think of was that it was too bad he didn't get immunity. If he had, maybe he would have backed you up on everything! Maybe he would have even admitted everything."

I didn't believe that would have happened under any circumstances. McGwire was protecting his legacy, and he was still expecting to get into the Hall of Fame. He was the single-season home-run king, and he didn't want to see that record tarnished or even thrown out entirely. Plus there might have been legal consequences. I'd been out of the game for a long time, and I was still worried that they might bust me for telling the truth; McGwire had only recently retired, and—immunity or not—somebody, somewhere, would have found some way to nail him.

As dinner drew to a close, Rob opened up. "I didn't tell you this before, Jose, but when we first walked into that room this morning, to face those congresspeople, I really believed that our friends in Florida were going to try to find a way of putting you back in jail."

"And you let me walk in there!"

"It turned out okay, didn't it? I know you were nervous, but there wasn't a single question you didn't handle well."

"That's because you told me what to say," I said.

"I just gave you a little guidance. But it was all based on the truth, and that made it easy."

"Easy?" I laughed. "Maybe for you!"

"How about that Congressman Davis?"

"Well, he kept his word, anyway."

"He knew I was ready to walk."

"So was I," I said.

"It's a good thing we didn't. You did an honorable thing, Jose. And we're going to see results."

That night, I got a call from my ex-wife, Jessica. "You did great," she said.

It was nice to hear something positive from her. It hadn't been the friendliest divorce in the history of the United States, but we got along pretty well, especially lately. "I did okay, didn't I?" I said, fishing for compliments.

"Yeah," she said, but her mind was on other things: "What is wrong with those fucking guys? They were lying to Congress!"

"Tell me about it."

"I was there when you were sticking needles in their asses! Aren't they worried about going to jail for lying?"

"I don't know," I said. "But that was one thing I didn't have to worry about. I have never lied about any of this, and I never will."

In the days and weeks ahead, more and more people began to take my side, and many of them did it on the record. "There's no question that Canseco was vindicated by testimony in Washington," one reporter noted. "I just remember vividly watching McGwire's performance and seeing Canseco sitting there, and thinking just how, amazingly, these two guys had changed places."

Then there was the *Miami Herald*, which not all that long ago had called me an "attention-starved 'roidhead," and worse. Now Kevin Baxter, a staff reporter, was writing, "After Mark McGwire's pathetic performance before the Congressional committee investigating steroid use in baseball last week, can anyone doubt Canseco's claims that McGwire used performance-enhancing drugs? After one committee member confronted commissioner Bud Selig with a 10-year-old quote about steroids in baseball, can anyone doubt Canseco's claims that baseball knew it had a steroid problem 10 years ago and chose to look the other way? And after a committee subpoena revealed baseball's new get-tough drug-testing policy has more holes than the Kansas City Royals' infield, can anyone doubt Canseco's charge that baseball cannot be trusted to police itself when it comes to performance-enhancing substances?

"Just because we don't like the messenger doesn't mean we should dismiss the message. Sure Curt Schilling looked more confident and composed than Canseco, but when he told the committee drug use was not a problem in baseball, he not only strained credulity, he also contradicted his strongly held views from just a few years ago.

"In contrast, Canseco's ill-fitting suit, bloodshot eyes and greased-back hair gave him the sincerity of a Mafia don. But when he said 'baseball did nothing to take [drugs] out of the sport. Baseball owners and the players union . . . turned a blind eye to the clear evidence of steroid use in baseball,' he might have come closer to the truth than anyone else on the panel."

Baxter had more to say, and all of it was dead-on: Steroids were tolerated in baseball because they served baseball's interests. And the owners knew all about it. But they did nothing because they'd been hurting since the 1994 strike, and these big guys on the field, breaking records with their moon shots, were bringing the fans back.

Four seasons later, McGwire and Sammy Sosa were chasing Roger Maris's single-season home-run record, and the whole world was watching. "Charges that both had used performance-enhancing drugs were either ignored or drowned out by the whirring of turnstiles and the ringing of cash registers," Baxter wrote.

Finally, people were beginning to tell the truth, and to *believe*. But there was so much more to tell. Why, for example, had Congress failed to call on most of the players I'd named in my book? And what about the players I hadn't named . . . ?

Not long after the hearings, to satisfy the demands of Congress, Major League Baseball hired one of its own, former U.S. senator George J. Mitchell, to launch a so-called investigation into the steroid scandal. It had a great title: *Report to the Commissioner of Baseball of an Independent Investigation into the Illegal Use of Steroids and Other Performance Enhancing Substances by Players in Major League Baseball.*

I found the use of the word *independent* more than a little suspect. Mitchell had been a consultant to the owners of the Boston Red Sox since 2002. He had served on the board of directors of the Florida Marlins. His law firm had done legal work for the Major League Baseball Players Association. The report was bought and paid for by Major League Baseball. And so on and so forth. I think you get my drift. It's about as independent as if Simon Cowell voted for his own son on *American Idol*.

In mid-April, I was invited to speak at the University of Florida, in Gainesville, by David Buchalter, then chairman of the Accent Speakers Bureau. I worked hard on that speech, and I will admit that I got plenty of help with it, but I am proud of it, and I hope you will humor me by allowing me to include portions of it here.

Never in my wildest dreams could I have imagined that my life and athletic ability would lead me down a path even close to what I have experienced over the last few months.

As I am sure you can imagine, what I thought would be a simple book about my life has kept me extremely busy. Interviews, contracts, appearing before Congress, and of course the confirmation of my book's success by my recent appearance on *The Surreal Life.* I am thankful for the chance to speak in a forum where TV cameras are not recording, reporters aren't hammering me with questions, and flashbulbs are not exploding.

When I decided to write my life's story, I was aware that what I revealed about myself and the game I played for a majority of my life would create a stir in the athletic world. When my book was released I was questioned regarding my motives, my truthfulness, and endured endless attacks on my family and my personal life. . . .

I was born with my twin brother to humble beginnings on July 2, 1964, in Regla, Cuba. People in our small town would say that Ozzie and I were like pocket-size atom bombs when we were babies. Although twins were not unusual in Cuba at the time, for twins to survive birth and early life was. Those were very difficult and turbulent times as the Cuban government was aware that my father did not support their system and desperately wanted to leave Cuba for a better life in the United States.

One year after I was born the Cuban government announced that it would allow an airlift of people. So our small family went to the airport hoping to be one of the lucky groups that were permitted to leave. When we arrived, there was only one plane that held about twenty people. Somehow we were chosen and my family, along with a few other people, packed ourselves into the tiny prop-engine plane for the trip to the United States.

I do not remember much of the trip, but was reminded as a young boy of the importance of the journey and how fortunate we were to have escaped Cuba. My father told us how hot the plane was and how difficult it was to leave behind the home he had created in Cuba prior to Castro coming to power. We left behind family, friends, money, personal possessions, and took with us only hope and uncertainty of a better life.

We had nothing. No home, no job, no idea of our future. But my father had experience teaching English, which allowed him to land a job with Amoco Oil. It was good position, but still he had to work extra jobs as a security guard at night to supplement our family's income. As a result my father rarely had extra time to spend with his two boys.

The one thing that we did do with my father was play baseball. On afternoons between jobs Dad would drive Ozzie and me to a nearby school in Opa-locka so he could teach us baseball. This began when we were about three or four years old and continued for years. We could hardly wait until school would get out so that we could hit baseballs against any backdrop, wall or field. I had no idea that this beginning would play such an important role in where my life would go.

As a young boy I had continuous health problems. Degenerative bone problems with my back, scoliosis, and generally a hard time recovering from any strenuous activity. I remember later in my life coming home from baseball practice or games and having to lie on the floor so that my back could straighten out and the pain would go away. This is probably why my father said that Ozzie took to the game faster than I did. I could always hit the ball further, but Ozzie seemed to have a quicker ability to move laterally when we were younger.

Back then my father used a little-known system of negative/positive reinforcement. Basically instead of offering words of encouragement like "Great hit," or "You are going to be great," he would say, "You are going to grow up and work at Burger King or McDonald's," or "You will never amount to anything." In my father's mind this negative/positive encouragement would make us work harder to prove him wrong. Kind of a reverse psychology of improvement for young kids. I still remember his favorite negative/positive reinforcement term when he would shout lovingly to us, "You stink!" It must have worked, because even though it was hard to take as a young child it continued to motivate me to do better to prove him wrong, and it still sticks with me to this day.

While my father got me started on a baseball track, it was my mother who provided me with everything else. When Dad's comments would upset us, Mom would make us feel better. She was a stay-at-home mom who had a way of healing anything that hurt. I never saw her ever being angry with us, not once, even though sometimes we definitely deserved it.

Mom never came to our games. That was our father's domain. My mother was our rock. She was our protector when my dad had a bad day at work or [got mad for] some other reason. Although it may be hard to believe, I was not always an angel and sometimes I deserved discipline. My mom was the one who was always trying to soften the blows from Dad. It was evidently clear to me that I was closer to my mom and loved her very much.

People find it hard to believe, but I always wanted to do something other than baseball when I was growing up. I loved going to the movies and remember watching Bruce Lee in *Enter the Dragon*. I could not wait to copy his moves and hopefully get into the movies.

As I said before, we had nothing. There was no extra money for private lessons, or to even attend a proper martial arts class. But where there is a will there is a way, and we found a friend who knew an instructor who agreed to teach us some of the moves we had seen. Although the lessons were sporadic, Ozzie and I constantly practiced with each other. As a result, over the next twenty years I became proficient in three different martial arts. The discipline associated with the martial arts helped me in many ways later in life.

That was how my early life developed. I spent time playing baseball, working on martial arts, and trying to live a dream that always seemed just beyond the reach of a Cuban-born immigrant. Pedro Gomez, who covered the Oakland A's for years, recalled that I was like the Judd Nelson character in *The Breakfast Club.* The guy that the principal kept turning the screws into so he could get a smart-ass response. I just never knew when to turn it off. I like to think that my attitude just reflected how comfortable I was with myself. As the author Michael Chabon recently wrote in the *New York Times,* "I've never seen a man who seems more comfortable with who he is than Jose Canseco. Not with who we think he is, like our current president, or with his best idea of himself, like our president's predecessor, but with himself."

Needless to say, with such a less-than-great beginning I was shocked to get drafted into baseball in 1982. I began my career in Idaho Falls. Again, we had no money. I was making six hundred dollars per month. I had two pairs of jeans that I wore all the time when I wasn't in uniform. All the players lived together in a place that was almost condemned. We began calling it the Animal House. I was young and innocent as to the power behind the machine that was Major League Baseball.

I did not light the world on fire that first year. I barely hit .260. I began to think that I was wasting my time and that I should just give up and go back to Florida. Then I received a call from my sister that I needed to come home because my mom was sick. When I got to the hospital my mother had already suffered a brain aneurism brought on by a blood clot in her back. She was in a coma. The doctor told us that her brain was dead and that was it.

I stayed with my mom in the hospital and even though I knew she was already gone, I told her then that I was going to be the best athlete in the world. No matter what it would take I was going to be the best. I knew she could hear me. I felt it in my soul. Then she was gone.

I will be the first to admit that up to that point I never really worked very hard at baseball. Everything changed that day. I worked harder, stayed later, and was determined to find each and every little helper that I could to make me the best athlete and fulfill the promise I made to my mother. When I found out about steroids it seemed like the answer to my prayers and the best way for me to accomplish what I had promised to my mom.

People always talk about how steroids make you a cheater. I guess to some extent that is true. But what they fail to acknowledge is that steroids, or any other drug or aid, do not give you talent. They do not give you eye-hand coordination. They cannot create what you do not have to begin with. Did steroids improve my ability to do the things that I could already do? Most certainly. But I also firmly believe that my own natural talent and ability, together with my personal drive to succeed, would have resulted in a great professional baseball career.

The common misconception is that taking steroids is a guarantee of success. That cannot possibly be true. Jason Giambi had a miserable season in 2004, way below his lifetime batting average of .302. Ken Caminiti, myself, and others who have taken steroids have seen our careers go up and down, just as any other athlete who may not take steroids. There is no guarantee of success. You must work harder, train harder, eat better, and generally do more when you take steroids than at any other time when you do not.

Why then do athletes choose to expose themselves to the risks and uncertainties? I wish the answer was simple. In most cases the answer is surprisingly not for the fame and the money. While some may take them hoping to get an advantage, the plain answer is that most do it just to survive in their sport. While Jason Giambi and Barry Bonds are regular All-Stars, if you are to believe me and the late Ken Caminiti, more than half of the players in baseball are taking steroids today. They are not All-Stars and are doing it just to stay in the game and pay the bills.

It is clear that technology has moved at lightning speed. In the world of genetics, which includes the chemistry associated with steroids, we have seen gene-splicing, test-tube babies, cloning, and even the ability to change the sex and makeup of children while still in the womb. Technology permits Tiger Woods to see and correct his athletic performance. Permits sprinters to wear lighter clothing and cyclists to alter physical characteristics to enhance their athletic performance. We accept these enhancements but do not accept chemical assistance.

The reality is that we need to address this issue. The time has come to end the secrecy that has existed in the sporting world for years and to confront those who refuse to acknowledge their role in encouraging the behavior the fans and public seem so interested in.

I then talked about some of the things I'd shared earlier with Congress—the pressure that made players turn to steroids, the need for honest answers, the importance of getting a commitment to fix the problem from someone other than the people who were running baseball—and I closed by saying that I hoped my book would finally accomplish what I had set out to accomplish: cleaning up the game.

Later that month, I flew back to Florida yet again, this

time for a trial. If you read my first book, you might remember that story: On Halloween night, 2001, I was at a Miami bar with my brother, Ozzie. He had his fiancée with him, and I'd brought a date, and a jerk grabbed my date's ass, and things almost got a little crazy. I say *almost* because nothing much happened. I didn't hit anybody, and Ozzie basically put his hands on the guy to protect himself. But then the asshole's friends got involved, and Ozzie had to take care of them. He knows martial arts, just like me, and he had to throw a couple of punches in self-defense.

The cops showed up, asked a few questions, spoke to a few eyewitnesses, then determined that nothing much had happened and sent us on our way. Less than two weeks later, I was sued by the guys we had fought and faced charges of aggravated battery, and my appearance in a Florida courtroom was the culmination of years of legal bullshit.

The opposing counsel began by referring to my book, specifically to a passage in which I had written about my early childhood fascination with Bruce Lee, the martial artist. Somehow this made me a violent person. Then he used my recent appearance before Congress to paint a picture of me as opportunistic and dishonest. (There it was again: *liar*.) It was amazing to me, and I sat there shocked and frustrated. I was 100 percent honest during my appearance at the hearings in front of Congress, and these bastards were trying to suck money out of me by using that honest testimony to paint me as a liar.

It went from bad to worse. If you've never been on trial,

I will tell you that it is both extremely unpleasant and extremely nerve-racking. You go in with the best attitude, determined to be forthright and honest, but as you look around—at the jury, at the battery of lawyers, at the judge—it becomes increasingly difficult to stay cool. It quickly became apparent that the trial was not a search for the truth, but a search for money. It was upsetting, yes, and I said some things I wish I could have taken back. I know Ozzie felt the same way, because we were both seriously worried when the jurors went off to deliberate. When they returned to the courtroom, not long afterward, we noticed that several of the women were crying, and we had no idea what to make of that. When the decision came down against us, however, I figured that the women had probably been pressured to find us liable. And that's exactly what they did. The court determined that Ozzie was liable for 90 percent of the so-called injuries, and that I was responsible for the remaining 10 percent. Then the other side moved to consolidate the judgment, which was a legal move to make us both liable for the full amount, $1.2 million. But I was the one with the money. Ozzie may have been liable, but everyone knew that the guy they'd be collecting from was me.

I was crushed. I felt the judgment made no sense at all. We were right, yet we had lost. I went into near isolation for a while, then August rolled around and brought a big surprise: it was revealed that Palmeiro had tested positive for stanozolol (the generic term for Winstrol, a synthetic anabolic steroid usually taken as a pill). People couldn't believe it, let alone explain it, but in my heart I know that my paranoid self had got it right. I can't prove this but I figured that Palmeiro had probably tested positive *prior* to the hearings, and the MLB brass had suppressed the findings, just as imagined. They couldn't afford the bad publicity, especially with the hearings coming up, so they had made that crazy deal with Palmeiro: *Deny deny deny, and we'll cover your ass.* That August, however, Mitchell and his team subpoenaed the test results—the *one* intelligent thing they'd done—and Major League Baseball was forced to come clean and release the findings.

And what gall the guy had! When Palmeiro left the hearings, knowing what he knew, knowing what he and MLB had been able to suppress, he was still trying to spin the story. "It turns out to be a positive thing that [Canseco] wrote this stupid book," he told reporters. "[If] he turns himself around, and if he can be a positive role model, I'll forgive him."

Forgive me? For what? Telling the truth?

What an idiot. The brass used him, then threw him under the bus.

I believe it was Congressman Davis who said, "You could've knocked me over with a feather when [Palmeiro] tested positive." Palmeiro knew he was a steroids user, and he knew I knew. Yet he stared down those congresspeople, wagged his little finger, and—with contempt dripping from his voice, into the chamber—unequivocally denied using steroids *and* called me out as a liar. Now here we were, only months after the hearings, and Rafi tests positive. Who's lying exactly?

Still, even when the results of Palmeiro's tests were

made public, nobody was running over to apologize for having called me a liar, or to congratulate me for telling the truth. Not that I had great expectations. I understand the system. I understand hypocrisy. I understand the bullshit. When they think I'm a liar, they'll scream it from the mountaintops. When they find out I'm telling the truth, nothing but silence.

Still, slowly but surely, the tide continued to turn.

Ray Ratto, the national columnist, wrote about the hearings in an August 1 column for ESPN.com: "I'll bet the next sentence you read is one you haven't read before: 'Hey, honey, have you seen my copy of *Juiced*?'

"Yes, the most maligned baseball book since the first printing of *Ball Four* may turn out to be just as important, because while Jose Canseco may be a certifiable nut case, he does seem to have one thing going for his first literary effort, namely this: He seems to be getting a lot of it right. . . . Imagine how insufferable Canseco is going to be when his nationwide 'Hey, I Told You So' tour begins."

Hey, I told you so. The tour begins when baseball opens the 2008 season, the first week of April. I can't wait.

In July 2005, Howard Bryant, a sportswriter from the *Boston Herald*, wrote *Juicing the Game: Drugs, Power, and the Fight for the Soul of Major League Baseball*. It was a pretty good book. Bryant talked about the 1998 season, when Mark McGwire and Sammy Sosa were vying for the home-run record, and, like the *Miami Herald*'s Kevin Baxter, pointed out how the battle had reignited interest in baseball. And baseball needed it, because the game had been in a terrible slump since the 1994 strike. The reignited interest increased television ratings, increased attendance at baseball games around the league, increased revenue.

So, as I'd been telling them, everyone in baseball—well, four guys in five, anyway—juiced up. And the leadership did nothing about it. Why? Because the game was fun again. The fans were back. And the profits—hell, who could have imagined it! So why would the owners look to take steroids out of the game? Steroids were good for the game, if all you're interested in is television ratings, attendance, and profits. Owners have never been accused of caring for their players' health or being uninterested in revenues. Quite the opposite. If they can find a way to make more money, they do it. And steroids made them more money. Lots of it.

Looking back, I think the country had been in the grip of a collective delusion. People were wondering, foolishly, how the game had become so damn *big*, and they looked everywhere for explanations. Everywhere except where they should have been looking.

The ballparks were smaller, they said. The strike zone was smaller. The bats were better and more powerful. The new, high-compression baseballs were responsible. I remember seeing articles with pictures of a baseball sliced open, showing a cross section, explaining how the modern ball was more tightly wound and suggesting that it just *flew* off the bat on its own. Somebody even suggested that the players were finally doing their homework, that they were watching themselves on videotape and learning from their mistakes. And watching opposing pitchers on videotape so that they'd know what was coming. It was laughable! The entire analysis was laughable. The answer was clear, and any fool could sum it up in one word. That word was *steroids*. The only reason players were hitting home runs with more regularity, more consistency, and more power than at any other time in the history of the game was that steroids were giving them the edge. And it was a *magical* edge. With steroids, a player could perform at his peak, and *beyond,* for an entire season. Maintaining that performance over the entire season was key. The human body takes a hell of a beating in a season, but here was something that taught the body not to care! I'll take that, and make it a double!

Now that the cat was finally crawling out of the bag, baseball commissioner Bud Selig would be "defined by how this era is viewed in history," according to Howard Bryant, the *Boston Herald* reporter who wrote *Juicing the Game.* "I mean, you are looking at a baseball establishment that has said that it wanted to get rid of steroids for ten years, but I don't recall baseball ever doing a public service announcement, saying to kids, 'Hey, kids. This is bad for you.' I don't recall baseball ever doing an independent investigation. They haven't spent a penny, at least to my knowledge, to go out and investigate what is going on with this steroid business."

Man, that felt good! That's what I wanted to hear. That's why I'd written my book. And people were finally starting to acknowledge the truth.

Here's a small sampling:

Senator Jim Bunning, a Hall of Fame former pitcher:

"I observed people getting stronger and hitting more home runs as they got older. When I played baseball, just the opposite happened."

Chris Haft, *San Jose Mercury News:* "People knew that Jose Canseco and other players were using some sort of performance-enhancing substances as far back as the late eighties and early nineties, and yet nobody really did anything about it."

Jim Leyritz, retired MLB player: "We all knew what was going on in the game."

Mark Gonzales, *Chicago Tribune:* "Baseball needed some momentum. Home runs really got the game back on focus."

Senator Bunning again: "Major League Baseball was recovering from a dramatic strike. I think they were looking for any stimulant to get fans back."

Ray Ratto, columnist: "Baseball turned a blind eye because it was cashing checks, and check-cashing is always the most popular thing in baseball."

Charlie Jones, sportscaster: "If Jose Canseco does not write the book, then MLB has the same rules on drugs that they had five years ago, which means nothing."

And Tom Verducci of *Sports Illustrated* certainly changed his tune: "[Canseco's book] held up a mirror to baseball. Maybe that mirror was foggy, maybe every detail wasn't exactly right, but baseball needed to be called on it, and Canseco did that."

Thanks, Tom. *Finally.* And by the way, maybe you should write a whole new story about me, and how wrong you were? Or is that too much to ask?

Suddenly, everywhere I went, people were calling my name—in a *good* way—and high-fiving me. I had made the transition from leper to megastar in months. Baseball's dirty little secret was out. Let's give credit where credit is due.

Then the publisher called and asked if I would go back on the road. Sure. Why not? I went back to signing books again. To huge lines and huge sales.

One afternoon I saw Rickey Henderson's mother standing in line with the rest of the fans. When it was finally her turn, she gave me a big smile and congratulated me, then reached for her cell phone and dialed her son, one of the greatest base-stealers of all time.

"I'm standing in front of Jose Canseco. I want you to say hey to him." With that, she handed me the phone.

"Way to go, man!" Henderson said. "Great book! Congratulations!"

I'm not sure Rickey had actually read the book, but so what?—he got it right. It *was* a great book, *honest,* anyway. And I *did* deserve congratulations.

Another big change was that suddenly the media wanted to hear what I had to say. When the book came out, it was like "Shut the hell up, you liar!" Now they were actively seeking out my opinions. *No, I don't recommend steroids for everyone, and certainly not without the help of a professional. Maybe they have a place in professional sports, but I'm not sure what that is. No, I don't feel that by using steroids I was selling my soul to the devil—or maybe I do. I'll have to get back to you on that. And, yes, a lot of liars testified before Congress.*

It made me think of why I got into steroids in the first place, way back when I was no more than a kid, really, and how I had been determined to win at all costs. I had been taught to strive for greatness, and I certainly did, but maybe wanting to be the best, *at any cost,* wasn't the smartest approach. That phrase is what kills you: *at any cost.* You have to ask yourself if the price is going to be too high. And how the hell are you supposed to know that before you take the plunge? If you don't know the price, how can you figure out in advance whether it's too high? And maybe it isn't too high. Maybe it is exactly the price you should pay. Everyone is different. Everyone makes his or her own choices.

In November of 2005, fully nine months after my book was released, MLB finally passed a new drug policy. The Associated Press ran the story as follows:

> Major league players and owners agreed Tuesday to toughen penalties for steroid use to a 50-game suspension for a first failed test, 100 games for a second, and a lifetime ban for a third.
>
> Baseball also will test for amphetamines for the first time starting next year under the deal, which must be ratified by owners and players.
>
> Baseball's current steroid penalties are a 10-day suspension for a first offense, 30 days for a second offense, and 60 days for a third. The earliest a player could be banned for life is a fifth offense.
>
> "This is an important step to reaching our goal of ridding our sport of performance-enhancing sub-

stances and should restore the integrity of and public confidence in our great game," commissioner Bud Selig said in a statement. "I appreciate the effort put forward by the Players Association and our players in reaching this new agreement."

Well, it looked like the inmates were taking over the asylum. In my opinion, Selig is a clown and a hypocrite who does exactly what the owners tell him to do, which I guess is pretty much what he's paid to do. His job is to protect the owners' interests, to ensure that anything and everything that happens in Major League Baseball is first and foremost about them.

I tried not to be too cynical, but it was hard. If you gave it any real thought, it wasn't exactly progress. The owners were still in charge, and these were powerful guys who don't usually show their faces. I don't know if you saw the movie *The Natural*, with Robert Redford, but they got that part just right: In one scene the owner of the team actually makes an appearance, but he is standing in the background, in the shadows, only vaguely visible. But it's obvious that he's the one running the show. So I guess things hadn't changed much since the old days. The owners pulled the strings that made the Seligs of the world dance. The people you didn't see, faceless, dangerous men, wielded most of the real power.

Some interesting news came in mid-December, when federal law enforcement personnel searched the home of Kirk Radomski, a personal trainer who had once worked for the New York Mets. (This may have been the investigation that leaked shortly after my book was published, but I'm not sure about that, so please don't quote me.) Radomski had been suspected of selling steroids and other performance-enhancing drugs to professional baseball players, and those suspicions turned out to be well grounded. As the investigation continued and other trainers were implicated, plenty of players were caught up, including—believe it or not—Roger Clemens (although most of the names weren't made public until December 2007, with the release of the Mitchell Report).

Brian McNamee, a conditioning coach, was also named, along with a host of guys I'd crossed paths with over the years, including Lenny Dykstra, David Segui, Larry Bigbie, Brian Roberts, Jack Cust, Tim Laker, Josias Manzanillo, Andy Pettitte, Chuck Knoblauch, Jason Grimsley, and others—but I won't go on; I think you get the idea.

Clemens, of course, was of great interest to me, especially on the heels of his being excised from my book and from my subsequent media appearances. And he was still denying it, even as rumors began to circulate that he was going to be named in the Mitchell Report. At one point, not long after the report came out, I believe he said something about conducting an investigation of his own, to find the source of the terrible allegations, and I remember thinking, if what they said about Clemens was true, that was about on par with O. J. Simpson hunting the streets of Los Angeles for the *real* killers.

Of course, when the Mitchell Report was finally released, things suddenly looked pretty bad for Clemens.

The report said that a year after he signed with the Toronto Blue Jays, the club hired McNamee as its strength and conditioning coach. And McNamee had lots to say. He said, for example, that he had lunch at my Florida house in June 1998, and that Clemens had been there; and he said that at one point Clemens and some shady character and I had gone off to talk private business.

When the Blue Jays returned to Toronto, McNamee went on, he was approached by Clemens, who was apparently ready to do steroids but didn't have the cojones to inject himself. And so, McNamee said, he did it for him.

I thought this was interesting because, back in November 2006, McNamee had spoken to *Sports Illustrated* reporter Jon Heyman and told a completely different story. "I don't have any dealings with steroids or amphetamines," he said. "I didn't buy it, sell it, condone it, or recommend it. I don't make money from it, it's not part of my livelihood and not part of my business." So it was the age-old question *Were you lying then or are you lying now?*

How did Mitchell and his guys miss that article?

When McNamee spoke to the Mitchell Report investigators, he said he had injected Clemens in the buttocks on numerous occasions. The product was either Sustanon 250 or Deca-Durabolin, and it had apparently been obtained from Radomski, according to the Mitchell Report.

Now, I don't pretend to know what happened back in Toronto, but I'll tell you this: I do remember the party at my house—the one McNamee was talking about—because Clemens had been invited, but he failed to show.

"You missed a good party, man," I told him the next time I saw him.

"Yeah, I heard," he said. "I was playing golf."

"See if you ever get invited again," I said, but I was smiling.

After the Mitchell Report came out, I finally heard from one of my fellow players. It was Clemens, calling to tell me that the whole thing was bullshit. "Can you believe what these people are doing to me?" he said.

"Yeah, I can believe it," I said. "Nothing surprises me anymore. I do know that Mitchell got it wrong, though, especially that bit about the party. I know you were never there."

"That's exactly what I'm talking about!" he said. "McNamee is full of shit!"

I felt so bad for the guy that I fessed up and told him that I'd actually put his name in my book, and that the publisher had taken it out.

"Jesus, Jose! Really? What did you say about me? Did you say I'd done steroids?"

"No. I never saw you do steroids. I said I thought you might have been doing them, but I could have been wrong, and I would never make such a claim, about you or about anyone else, if I hadn't seen it with my own eyes."

"I'm going to sue all those motherfuckers for printing lies about me," Clemens said.

"That's what I would do. And if you need me to testify on your behalf, or for anything else, I'm here, man."

"Thanks, Jose. I really appreciate it."

"That's what friends are for."

There was a pause, and I was just about to ask him whom he had working for him behind the scenes—what mysterious powerhouse had managed to keep his name out of my book *and* off the air—but he'd already hung up.

4

THE POLYGRAPH TEST

For weeks on end, the media analyzed and overanalyzed the congressional hearings, but I didn't think there was all that much to analyze: I'd been honest and just about everyone else was full of shit. Meanwhile, I tried to get back to my normal life.

My daughter, Josie, ten at the time, always had the power to snap me out of my worst moods, and I really enjoyed hanging out with her. We would play semi-inappropriate video games, go to movies, or settle in for a night of my personal favorite, poker. I've turned her into a pretty good player, by the way, and that cute face is almost impossible to read.

Every now and then, Josie would be in some kind of school production, and I found myself really looking forward to those nights. I'd get a little nervous, too. When I arrived, I always felt like nudging the parent next to me and saying, "You see that beautiful little girl up there?—no, not that one, the *most* beautiful one—that's my daughter." But I didn't nudge anyone because I'm not the most social guy in the world. And people didn't generally approach me, either, because I'm big, and maybe they find me a little intimidating. Or maybe it relates to that unwritten rule in the greater Los Angeles school district: *If there's a celebrity parent in your class, be cool. Let him or her be a parent.*

When Josie and I are out in public, however, it is a different story. I'm pretty big, as I said—six-four, 240 pounds—so people notice me, and they seem to have no qualms about hurrying over and introducing themselves. I've tried hiding under a cap and dark glasses, but that only makes them look harder. (This is Hollywood, after all, and that getup is pretty much a cry for attention.) Funnily enough, even people who don't recognize me think I'm *somebody,* so they'll come over and ask me point-blank, "Do I know you from somewhere?" or, "Are you an actor or an athlete or something?"

"Yeah, I'm something," I might say.

"What?"

"I'm Jose Canseco."

Sometimes they'll say, "Jose who?" But mostly it hits them right away. And you know what's weird? They always go to the book first; that's what they talk about: The Book. It's as if my baseball career never existed, not the Most Valuable Player award, not the Rookie of the Year award, not my 40-40 season, not my largest-in-history baseball contract—none of it. On the other hand, to look on the bright side, I guess I have successfully redefined myself as a writer. I've gone from *Most Valuable Player* to *Number One New York Times Bestselling Author Jose Canseco.* It's a mouthful, but it does have a nice ring.

But there's another funny thing: A lot of times, when I tell people who I am, their heads kind of snap back in amazement. "No, you're not!" they'll say. "You *can't* be Jose Canseco."

"I can't?" I'll say. "How come?"

"He's *old,* man!"

I don't know what they're thinking—I'm only forty-three—but I guess when you leave the game (or the game leaves you), the assumption is that you're ready for the grave. As one of my friends put it, "After you retire, your life is measured in dog years, so they expect you to be an old fuck, not a baby-faced hulk."

Baby-faced hulk? Okay, I'll take that. I've been called worse.

I try to spend as much time with my daughter as I can, and now that she's a near teenager I'm beginning to get a little nervous. Josie is strong-willed, just like her mother, Jessica, and when she wants something, she usually gets it. She wants to go bowling, we go bowling. She wants to ride horses, off we go to ride horses. I'm not looking forward to the day she discovers boys, but at least I've got size on my side. I don't imagine too many boys are going to ignore me when I say, "Please have my daughter home by eleven."

That same posthoopla year, 2006, I went off and redefined myself yet again, this time on television, as part of *The Surreal Life,* the crazy VH1 show. I don't know why I did it, frankly. Boredom, maybe? Or maybe just to keep myself busy while this whole scandal continued to play itself out. It turned out to be interesting, though. I'm a bit of a loner, as I've said, and I need my space, and there I was, stuck in a house for twelve days with a bunch of strangers. No phone, no TV, nothing. And of course every day the producers would create weird new stuff for us to do. I think my housemates were a little surprised by how quiet I was, because, as a ballplayer, or a former ballplayer, anyway, I'm expected to be a wild and crazy guy. But I'm a genuine introvert, and I think people got to see a side of me they never knew existed. Of course I'm guessing some people probably thought I was just boring. But I honestly enjoyed it. I was forced to socialize, and some of those people weren't half-bad. I liked Janice Dickinson, for example, the former supermodel, who seems to live life harder and faster and louder than the rest of us—but especially *louder*. Maybe she didn't get much attention as a kid. And I liked Omarosa, who'd been on *The Apprentice* and proved to be a smart lady. And I especially liked the combination of those two: watching Janice and Omarosa get into their little catfights was entertaining; maybe not for viewers at home, but it was certainly good enough for me. I love new experiences and trying new things. This was definitely a new experience, and interesting to live through.

On the last day of shooting, I had a couple of beers. I don't drink much, so I guess everyone thought a little booze might loosen me up. They were right. I ended up stripping down to my leopard-print underwear, to the delight of the producers. Would I do it again? The show, I mean, not the stripping. Hey, we're not talking steroids here: the answer is yes. To *both*.

In March 2006, an article in *Sports Illustrated* named me as a customer of some outfit called Applied Pharmacy Services. Maybe my memory was spotty, but that didn't ring a bell. The magazine said that I had also purchased stanozolol and HCG (human chorionic gonadotropin), along with a few hundred syringes, from an antiaging clinic that was no longer in business. My lawyer, Rob, was under the impression that I had never purchased any substances over the Internet, ever, but in fact I had, and we straightened out that little misunderstanding, honestly, and left it alone.

"Why the hell are we bothering to try and fix this?" I said. "That was in the past, and I'm no longer in the game."

"Things are heating up. They're digging into everything, and they're going to dig pretty deep."

"Well, I've got nothing to hide," I said. "I never did."

"You don't have to tell me."

"And you'd think they'd have bigger fish to fry. This fish got pulled from the water long ago."

The one thing that really bothered me, and kept bothering me, was that I hadn't heard anything from Mitchell's people. Not only had I been honest in my book and during the hearings, but I seemed to be emerging from the whole sordid mess more or less intact, with my credibility fully restored. And I had so much more to tell them. About some of the players I'd already mentioned in my book, and about some of the ones I hadn't mentioned.

Finally, in late March or early April 2006, I got a call from somebody with the investigation. I put them in touch with Rob, and a couple of weeks later we went to meet the investigators in an Embassy Suites Hotel in Santa Ana, Orange County, California. There was a lead attorney and a young guy, and I wasn't all that impressed by either of them. I felt I was being marginalized. I had written a book that had helped blow the lid off the whole steroids scandal, and I was trapped in a hotel room with two guys who didn't seem all that interested in hearing what I had to say.

I told them everything I'd already said in the book, and I added details. I even added names. The two guys listened, took notes from time to time, and every once in a while they would nod their heads politely.

Two hours later, Rob and I were in the car, heading back to Los Angeles. "Those guys weren't taking me seriously," I said.

"You don't know that," Rob said. "Maybe that's just the way they are."

"What way?"

"Types of guys who play it close to the vest."

"Don't give me that. They were just going through the motions! They just nodded. They only put in the time so they could say they had talked to me."

"Okay," Rob said. "Maybe you're right. Maybe they don't give a shit."

We subsequently got another call from someone w⟨⟩ ing for Mitchell's camp, asking if I'd be available fo⟨⟩ follow-up interview, and we agreed to meet with them ar⟨⟩ time, anywhere, but nothing came of it. I don't know wh⟨⟩ they even bothered to call.

Much later, Senator Mitchell claimed that in the weeks and months following the congressional hearings, he had personally called all the players connected to the scandal, to see if they knew anything that might shed more light on the investigation. Maybe he called a lot of the players, and maybe, for all I know, he called every single one of them, but Mitchell never called me. The only reason he was even "investigating" was because of my book. With everything I knew about the problem, I should have been a more central part of the investigation, not some guy who got subjected to rudimentary questions by a second-tier team that wasn't even interested in hearing what I had to say. In retrospect, I think Mitchell's men were basically going through the motions to cover their asses. "Yeah, we talked to Jose," they could say. "We did our work. He didn't have much to say."

The bottom line, in my opinion, is that they didn't want to hear from me. Or they'd heard enough. Or they had already made up their minds about whom they wanted to see, and what they wanted to hear, and neither I nor most of the guys in my book were considered to be particularly significant.

I'd been Mitch-slapped.

Frankly, from where I was sitting, it was starting to

look as if the whole thing was some kind of controlled scam, or, worse, a bad joke. After all, the Mitchell Report was basically financed by the very people it was supposed to be investigating, so it wasn't exactly credible. What good was that going to do anyone? What kind of results could we really expect?

And I was still angry. *Liar liar liar!* That still rankled. It rankled deep.

Then one afternoon, I had an epiphany. I was going to do something to clear my name once and for all. I decided I would take a lie-detector test. I would find the best guy in the business and subject myself to an honest-to-God, no-bullshit polygraph exam. I'd answer all the questions about my honesty through the best scientific means available. I'd end all doubt so that no one could ever again say that I'd lied.

As I began to look into it, though, I discovered that there were two very different approaches to the whole lie-detecting business, and if I was going to do it right, I'd be wise to subject myself to both. I didn't need anyone telling me, "Well, yeah, sure, but the *other* system is more scientific!" I didn't know which was more scientific, and I didn't even know what that meant, exactly, but I wasn't going to take any chances. I was going to do this right. I wasn't going to give the media or anyone else any opportunity to discredit me.

I looked for the two best guys in the business. The first guy I found was Jack Trimarco, of Jack Trimarco and Associates. He had been a polygraph examiner (also known as a forensic psychophysiologist, as I discovered)

for twenty-one years, and he had also served as a special agent for the FBI. He'd been in charge of the Los Angeles Field Office Polygraph Unit from 1990 until 1998, when he left the FBI. He had conducted 2,500 polygraph tests throughout the world and had helped in a wide range of investigations, going back to the Unabomber, Whitewater, the Oklahoma City bombing, and the 1993 bombing of the World Trade Center, so I figured he must be pretty good. It would be hard to argue that this guy wasn't an amazing expert in the field of polygraphs.

The first thing he had me do was to sit though a pretest interview, which, strangely enough, was longer than the test itself. I was nervous, but I tried to relax in the comfort that all I had to do was tell the truth. To eliminate all doubt, I had a friend videotape the entire proceedings from start to finish.

Jose, you're here to do a polygraph exam this morning. Can you tell me what it's about, and why you want to do this?

Jose: Well, to tell the truth, to finally let the fans know and the public know what really happened in the polygraph examination, which is the ultimate tell. Um, I'm here to talk about Mark McGwire, I injected him; Rafael Palmeiro, I injected him; also add some other players I dealt with, which is Magglio Ordonez, Dave Martinez, and obviously Ivan Rodriguez, who I injected. All these individuals. And obviously Jason Giambi, which I never injected but he was part of that crew and he was using steroids.

What do you think having this sort of polygraph exam made public will do for you personally? How do you feel about that?

Jose: Well, I think, put everything to rest. Show the public finally I am telling the truth and that when Rafael Palmeiro testified before Congress and shook his finger and said, "I never used steroids," just to show what really happened, what the true story is.

What was going through your mind when Rafael Palmeiro looked at the camera and said that "I have never used steroids"?

Jose: Well, I knew, because I injected him and supplied him with actual steroids, that something had happened. I knew that, I think, Major League Baseball had gotten ahold of him. I truly believe that he conspired with Major League Baseball to testify against me because afterwards we found out that Rafael Palmeiro tested positive for steroids, but I definitely knew at that time that he tested positive before testifying in front of Congress, and I truly believe that Major League Baseball kind of colluded Rafael Palmeiro into saying, "You know what, if you testify against Jose Canseco, we will not give these results to the actual media. You're very close to acquiring five hundred home runs and three thousand base hits"—which at that time there were only three or four players that accomplished that—"and for the exchange of testifying before Congress against Jose Canseco, we will hide these results." And that definitely happened. Now, what Rafael Palmeiro didn't take into account, that Congress got very smart, decided to go straight to the laboratories who actually these results were sent to, these results were brought back, Major League Baseball had these results in their hand, and kind of knew that Congress was gonna come after Major League Baseball and the results, gave it to the media, and there you go: Rafael Palmeiro tested positive for steroids.

If you were to meet with him today and talk with him about what had happened and what you think he ought to do, what do you think you would say to him?

Jose: I would say, "Hear me out for about an hour, and, you know, let's talk about what really happened. Let's try to get on the same page, let's try to tell the truth." And you know, I truly believe that Rafi's a victim in this, and I truly believe that Major League Baseball manipulated and controlled him. I'm prepared to back up the book one hundred percent, prepared to say I injected these players, you know, Mark McGwire, Rafael Palmeiro, and so forth.

So, just to be really clear, you're going to say that you injected Mark McGwire—

Jose: Absolutely.

You're going say that you injected Rafael Palmeiro?

Jose: Yes.

You're going to say that you injected Juan Gonzalez?

Jose: Yes.

You're going to say that you injected Ivan Rodriguez?

Jose: Yes.

You're going to say that you injected Dave Martinez?

Jose: Yes.

You're going to say that you injected Magglio Ordonez?

Jose: Yes.

And that you have personal knowledge of the fact that Jason Giambi has used steroids?

Jose: Absolutely, yes.

Well, good luck in there.

Jose: Thank you, I appreciate it.

As soon as we were done, Trimarco hooked me to the armband and everything and started the actual test. This was the moment of truth, literally, and I was happy to be going through this, to finally put to rest the criticism.

Jose: I'm ready.

Okay, here we go. Are you sometimes known as Mr. Canseco?

Jose: Yes.

Regarding if the information in your book is completely true, do you intend to be truthful with me about that?

Jose: Yes.

Are you convinced that I won't ask you any surprise questions on this test?

Jose: Yes.

Is the information in your book completely true?

Jose: Yes.

Is the information in *Juiced* completely true?

Jose: Yes.

Are you sure that I won't try and trick you on this test?

Jose: Yes.

That will conclude the test, remain still.

Man, that was weird. I remember wondering how that could possibly be the whole test, but then I realized that he'd asked me the only question that really mattered: *Had I been completely honest in my book?* And that covered everything.

A short while later, with the video still rolling, Trimarco presented his findings: "The relevant question on this test was 'Is the information in your book completely true?' and 'Is the information in *Juiced* completely true?' and Jose passed the test. I'm about to fax these charts to San Francisco for an independent blind analysis of the charts, but I expect with the purity of these charts that they will be nondeceptive by any expert who cares to examine them."

Trimarco called me twenty-four hours later: the tests had been examined in San Francisco, and I had passed with flying colors.

It felt so good to have that behind me. I knew I hadn't been lying, and now I had science backing me up.

I did the next test with John Grogan, also in Los Angeles. He was a polygraph instructor with thirty years in the business, and the author of the massive, nationally distributed *Polygraph Training Guide*. And when I say massive,

I mean massive: I'm told the guide weighs thirty-five pounds.

I also videotaped those proceedings, and Grogan introduced himself to the camera: "My name's John Grogan. I'm a polygraph examiner with GroganPolygraph. I've been involved in the lie-detection industry for the last three decades." He explained his technique, which was considerably different from Trimarco's, then administered the test, which was also considerably different—and far longer—than Trimarco's had been. I was glad that I'd subjected myself to both types of tests, because their approaches to polygraphy were worlds apart.

Grogan explained that he was going to be measuring microscopic changes to my breathing, both upper and lower breathing, whatever the hell that meant, along with microscopic changes to my blood pressure and the volume of blood. He also had some kind of sweat monitor, which he attached to my right hand. "I'm going to be asking you ten questions, spaced out [by] twenty-five seconds," he said. "Make sure you answer 'Yes' or 'No' with just your mouth, not nodding your head, and no moving at all during the test. Everything's reading good, so I'm going to start."

Is today Thursday?

Jose: Yes.

Is your name Jose?

Jose: Yes.

Did you and Mark McGwire ever have conversations about the use of steroids or human growth hormones?

Jose: Yes.

Is your last name Canseco?

Jose: Yes.

Did you ever inject Mark McGwire with steroids or human growth hormones?

Jose: Yes.

In the last ten years, have you lied to benefit yourself financially?

Jose: No.

Is your shirt black?

Jose: Yes.

Did you ever educate Rafael Palmeiro regarding the use of steroids or human growth hormones?

Jose: Yes.

Did you ever inject Rafael Palmeiro with steroids or human growth hormones?

Jose: Yes.

When you were growing up, did you ever steal money from your parents?

Jose: Yes.

Did you ever educate Juan Gonzalez concerning the use of steroids or human growth hormones?

Jose: Yes.

Did you ever inject Juan Gonzalez with steroids or human growth hormones?

Jose: Yes.

Did you ever educate Juan Gonzalez concerning the use of steroids or human growth hormones?

Jose: Yes.

Okay you can move, that chart was collected well.

Jose: I just stole a couple quarters from my mom's purse once when I was a little kid. I said, "Well, better answer that one right."

Grogan continued, "Okay, the computer scoring agrees with my hand scoring. The computer says absolutely no deception indicated. Probability that he is lying is less than one percent. . . . People that are telling absolutely the entire truth on all four important questions on a chart, that's the only way to get a .01 score, which is like getting an A-plus in school. The opposite end would be ninety-nine; that's the worst you can fail. There's absolutely no deception on this chart. . . . He did answer all of the significant questions truthfully. Okay, we've collected this chart, the collection went well, I'm going to pull up a scoring screen for it. . . . Here's his chart. The questions about hormones and steroid use are the red numbered questions here and here, and there's two more out of sight. The computer's going to add up changes to all four of his tracings and give a number from .01 as the best to 99 would be the worst. And there's his score: 'No Deception Indicated—Probability of deception is less than one in a hundred.' That's the best that anybody can do. That indicates that there was no deception on any of the four questions asked about steroids or hormones. The computer doesn't know who's taking the test; it doesn't know race, religion, age. It's strictly by the body responses, and this examinee did very well on those questions. I'm also an expert on countermeasures, which is any attempt to change or trick polygraph results. None of those were used on this; we would catch them in a second. He did very well. The next questions will be two about Dave Martinez and two about Wilson Alvarez."

Did you ever educate Dave Martinez concerning the use of steroids or human growth hormones?

Jose: Yes.

Did you ever inject Dave Martinez with steroids or human growth hormones?

Jose: Yes.

In any past relationship, did you ever cheat on someone who loved you?

Jose: Yes.

Is today Thursday?

Jose: Yes.

Did you ever educate Wilson Alvarez concerning the use of steroids or human growth hormones?

Jose: Yes.

Did you ever inject Wilson Alvarez with steroids or human growth hormones?

Jose: Yes.

Besides anything connected to drug use, have you ever committed a crime and got away with it?

Jose: No.

Okay, you can move, that was another good chart collection.

Jose: Did you ever have sex with a goat? Maybe!

Okay, here's his chart. . . . Let's go to a scoring screen. Okay, here's his chart again. Again, "No Deception Indicated—Probability of deception is less than .01." That's the best that anybody can pass. . . . So I'll set it up for the next chart. Next chart would be two questions about Magglio Ordo—

Jose: Ordonez.

Ordonez, and then, did Alex Rodriguez ever approach you about acquiring steroids or human growth hormones, and thereafter, did you introduce Alex Rodriguez to someone who you knew supplied other athletes with steroids or human growth hormones.

Jose: Okay.

Is today Thursday?

Jose: Yes.

Is your name Jose?

Jose: Yes.

Did you educate Magglio Ordonez on growth hormone and steroid use?

Jose: Yes.

Is your last name Canseco?

Jose: Yes.

Did you inject Magglio Ordonez with growth hormone or steroids?

Jose: Yes.

When you were growing up, did you steal from somebody who blindly trusted you?

Jose: No.

Is your shirt black?

Jose: Yes.

Did Alex Rodriguez ever approach you about acquiring steroids or human growth hormones?

Jose: Yes.

Thereafter, did you introduce Alex Rodriguez to someone who you knew had supplied other athletes with steroids or human growth hormones?

Jose: Yes.

In a previous relationship, did you ever cheat on someone who loved you?

Jose: Yes.

Okay, you can move. Good chart collection. Again, a perfect score. Absolutely no lying on any of the four relevant questions. Did very well; this is a one hundred percent pass.

At that point, Grogan again turned to face the camera: "Mr. Canseco sat still, he answered honestly, and he passed with no problems. He just simply answered honestly, and there's not a chance that he's lying. He's one hundred percent telling the truth on all questions regarding human growth hormone and steroids. And the computer misses nothing, not the most smallest, insignificant tracings, and it also agreed. It gave him a .01 score on every chart, which is, if this was in school, would be an A-plus on every chart collected."

A-plus. Shit. If I'd only done that well in school, I'd probably *own* a baseball team today. But I got through the tests. I was two for two. Perfect scores. No deception whatsoever.

Anyone who was still calling me a liar could take it up with those two guys.

And you can kiss my A-plus ass.

JOSE CANSECO

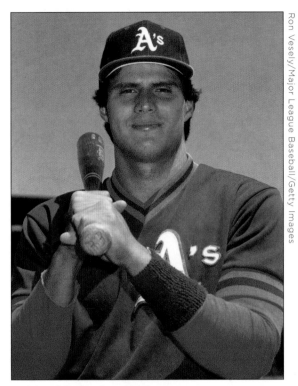

Oakland Athletics, 1985

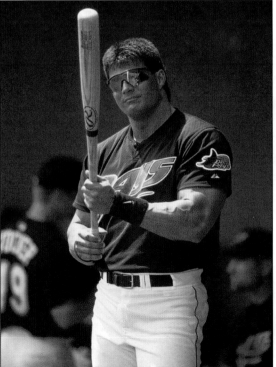

Tampa Bay Devil Rays, 2000

MARK McGWIRE

Bernstein Associates/Getty Images Sport/Getty Images

© Reuters/Corbis

Oakland Athletics, 1986

St. Louis Cardinals, 2001

SAMMY SOSA

Jonathan Daniel/Getty Images Sport/Getty Images

Mike Fiala/AFP/Getty Images

Chicago White Sox, 1990

Chicago Cubs, 2002

JUAN GONZALEZ

Joe Patronite/Getty Images Sport/Getty Images

Brian Bahr/Getty Images Sport/Getty Images

Texas Rangers, 1989

Texas Rangers, 1998

MIGUEL TEJADA

David Seelig/Getty Images Sport/Getty Images

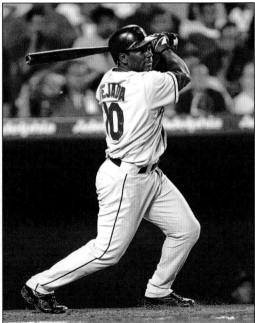

Stephen Dunn/Getty Images Sport/Getty Images

Oakland Athletics, 1997

Baltimore Orioles, 2004

BARRY BONDS

Pittsburgh Pirates, 1986

San Francisco Giants, 2003

ROGER CLEMENS

Boston Red Sox, 1984

Houston Astros, 2005

MAGGLIO ORDONEZ

Otto Greule Jr./Getty Images Sport/Getty Images

Chicago White Sox, 1998

Mark Cunningham/Major League Baseball/Getty Images

Detroit Tigers, 2007

ALEX RODRIGUEZ

Seattle Mariners, 1994

New York Yankees, 2007

My buddy Clemens and me during my three-month stint with the Yankees organization in 2000

That's me, in front of Congress, telling the whole truth and nothing but the truth.

5

THE MITCHELL REPORT

In March 2006, *Game of Shadows* hit the bookstores, which further fueled the ongoing steroid scandal. The book was subtitled *Barry Bonds, BALCO, and the Steroids Scandal that Rocked Professional Sports,* which pretty much summed it up. It was written by Mark Fainaru-Wada and Lance Williams, a pair of reporters from the *San Francisco Chronicle* who had been chasing the story for several years. I didn't read the book, but I heard it was pretty good, and I was happy that some media guys were finally doing some actual digging. I was told they had plenty of details about undetectable designer steroids, about the supplement industry in general, and about the way the suppliers had their tentacles in professional baseball and plenty of other sports.

Somebody told me that they even wrote about that Big

League Challenge in Las Vegas, where I ran into Bonds, who was so impressed with my physique that his eyes practically popped out of his head. In my version of the story, Bonds had told me that I looked ripped. In their version, he was equally impressed, but his words were different. "Dude," he reportedly said. "Where did you get all that muscle?"

I believe I had it right. I was there.

From what I heard, they went on to write about Bonds's evolution, and his "impressive musculature," and they said he was an especially big fan of growth hormone. Well, I don't know what was on his menu, but I can tell you this: I was there when he decided it was time to start, and I watched as he showed up months later with all that new muscle.

On the heels of this, former Red Sox pitcher Paxton Crawford admitted in an article in *ESPN The Magazine* that he had used steroids and human growth hormone in 2000 and 2001. He was quoted as saying that some of the players were walking around like zombies. Now, I don't doubt that some players were walking around like zombies, but I never saw them, and if they were, I don't believe it was connected to steroids. Maybe those guys were zombies to begin with. Steroid use doesn't make you walk around like a zombie. Still, I wasn't complaining. Every time a player came forward, or there was news of yet another steroid sting, it made me less of a liar, it bolstered my credibility, and it made me feel more and more, well, vindicated.

Finally, on December 13, 2007, the Mitchell Report was released. As the guy who started the thing, I flew to New York because I thought it was important for me to be there, but I wasn't permitted past the doors. I was told that the conference was only open to members of the press, which sounded like complete bullshit to me. Mitchell simply didn't want me there. He was probably worried that I'd steal his thunder. I'm sure he also knew that I would be the first player to read and evaluate his report. But nothing I could say or do would get me past the security guards at the door.

Once again, I'd been Mitch-slapped.

When I finally got around to reading the report, I was impressed that the investigative team had named a hundred players, including five MVPs, but I also noticed that many of the names in my book were nowhere in evidence. That seemed insane! It didn't sound as if these guys had been particularly thorough in their investigation. Theoretically, the report was supposed to be the result of an exhaustive investigation, leaving no stone unturned, yet they hadn't even bothered to look into the allegations I'd made in my bestselling book.

Still, I decided to give the report a fair chance—which was more than MLB ever did for me—and I plunged in. This is how the report began:

> For more than a decade there has been widespread illegal use of anabolic steroids and other performance-enhancing substances by players in

Major League Baseball, in violation of federal law and baseball policy. Club officials routinely have discussed the possibility of such substance use when evaluating players. Those who have illegally used these substances range from players whose major league careers were brief to potential members of the Baseball Hall of Fame. They include both pitchers and position players, and their backgrounds are as diverse as those of all major league players.

The response by baseball was slow to develop and was initially ineffective, but it gained momentum after the adoption of a mandatory random drug testing program in 2002. That program has been effective in that detectable steroid use appears to have declined. But the use of human growth hormone has risen because, unlike steroids, it is not detectable through urine testing.

This report, the product of an intensive investigation, describes how and why this problem emerged. We identify some of the players who were caught up in the drive to gain a competitive advantage through the illegal use of these substances. Other investigations will no doubt turn up more names and fill in more details, but that is unlikely to significantly alter the description of baseball's "steroids era," as set forth in this report.

From hundreds of interviews and thousands of documents we learned enough to accurately describe that era. While this investigation was prompted by revelations about the involvement of players with the Bay Area Laboratory Co-Operative, the evidence we uncovered indicates that this has not been an isolated problem involving just a few players or a few clubs. It has involved many players on many clubs. In fact, each of the thirty clubs has had players who have been involved with performance-enhancing substances at some time in their careers.

The illegal use of these substances was not limited to the players who are identified in this report. There have been many estimates of use. In 2002, former National League Most Valuable Player Ken Caminiti estimated that "at least half" of major league players were using anabolic steroids. Dave McKay, a longtime coach for the St. Louis Cardinals and the Oakland Athletics, estimated that at one time 30 percent of players were using them. Within the past week, the former Cincinnati Reds pitcher Jack Armstrong estimated that between 20 percent and 30 percent of players in his era, 1988 to 1994, were using large doses of steroids while an even higher percentage of players were using lower, maintenance doses of steroids. There have been other estimates, a few higher, many lower, all impossible to verify.

However, it is a fact that between 5 and 7 percent of the major league players who participated in anonymous survey testing in 2003 tested positive for performance enhancing substances. Those figures almost certainly understated the actual level of use since players knew they would be tested at some time during the year, the use of human growth hormone was not detectable in the tests that were conducted, and, as many have observed, a negative test does not necessarily mean that a player has not been using performance-enhancing substances.

Mandatory random testing, formally started in 2004 after the survey testing results, appears to have reduced the use of detectable steroids, but players switched to human growth hormone precisely because it is not detectable. Players who use human growth hormone apparently believe that it assists their ability to recover from injuries and fatigue during the long baseball season; this also is a major reason why players used steroids.

Okay, they were off to a promising start. I felt that this was accurate information, and I was hopeful the rest of the report was as candid.

Further along, I came to this:

The illegal use of performance-enhancing substances poses a serious threat to the integrity of the game. Widespread use by players of such substances unfairly disadvantages the honest athletes who refuse to use them and raises questions about the validity of baseball records.

In addition, because they are breaking the law, users of these substances are vulnerable to drug dealers who might seek to exploit their knowledge through threats intended to affect the outcome of baseball games or otherwise.

The illegal use of these substances to improve athletic performance also carries with it potentially serious negative side effects on the human body. Steroid users place themselves at risk for psychiatric problems, cardiovascular and liver damage, drastic changes to their reproductive systems, musculoskeletal injury, and other problems. Users of human growth hormone risk cancer, harm to their reproductive health, cardiac and thyroid problems, and overgrowth of bone and connective tissue.

Apart from the dangers posed to the major league player himself, however, his use of performance-enhancing substances encourages young athletes to use those substances. Young Americans are placing themselves at risk of serious harm. Because adolescents are already subject to significant hormonal changes, the abuse of steroids and other performance-enhancing substances can have more serious effects on them than they have on adults.

Still pretty good, right? I was preparing to be impressed. They may not have been all that thorough, but they didn't completely disappoint. They were clearly on the right track, and I was beginning to think that Mitchell's ties to Major League Baseball hadn't colored the entire investigation.

Next, I came across a section where they began to spread the blame.

Obviously, the players who illegally used performance-enhancing substances are responsible for their actions. But they did not act in a vacuum. Everyone involved in baseball over the past two decades—Commissioners, club officials, the Players Association, and players—shares to some extent in the responsibility for the steroids era. There was a collective failure to recognize the problem as it emerged and to deal with it early on. As a result, an environment developed in which illegal use became widespread.

And further along:

I was asked to investigate the use of performance-enhancing substances by major league players and to report what I found as fairly, as accurately, and as thoroughly as I could. I have done so.

Only the Commissioner is vested with authority to take disciplinary action. Any such determination is properly for the Commissioner to make, subject to the players' right to a hearing.

I urge the Commissioner to forego imposing discipline on players for past violations of baseball's rules on performance-enhancing substances, including the players named in this report, except in those cases where he determines that the conduct is so serious that discipline is necessary to maintain the integrity of the game. I make this recommendation fully aware that there are valid arguments both for and against it; but I believe that those in favor are compelling.

First, a principal goal of this investigation is to bring to a close this troubling chapter in baseball's history and to use the lessons learned from the past to prevent the future use of performance-enhancing substances. While that requires us to look back, as this report necessarily does, all efforts should now be directed to the future. That is why the recommendations I make are prospective. Spending more months, or even years, in contentious disciplinary proceedings will keep everyone mired in the past.

Okay. I wasn't going to argue with that. To punish players retroactively made no sense at all. But I did have a big problem further along:

The Commissioner should create a Department of Investigations, led by a senior executive who reports directly to the president of Major League Baseball. Ideally, this senior executive should have experience as a senior leader in law enforcement, with the highest credibility among state and federal law enforcement officials; the success of this department will depend in part upon how well it interacts with law enforcement authorities. The senior executive should have sole authority over all investigations of alleged performance-enhancing substance violations and other threats to the integrity of the game, and should receive the resources and other support needed to make the office effective.

Well, sure. That would make him another Bud Selig. Another puppet, listening for the voices in the shadows, jumping every time they jerked the strings. Mitchell was basically telling them to hire another guy they could control, another puppet beholden to their whims.

This is what they spent all that time and money on?

In places, the report missed the point entirely. For example, it praised MLB's labor relations department, noting that as a result of their efforts no work stoppages had occurred since the 1994 strike. "This fact, perhaps more than any other, explains why Major League Baseball today is on much firmer economic ground than it was just a decade ago," the report said.

Well, that was certainly a crock. The game was definitely on firmer economic ground than it had been in years, but that had nothing to do with labor relations, and everything to do with steroids. Steroids were putting asses in the seats, and the management bozos had nothing to do with it. It was us, the freaks on the field, hitting harder and faster than at any other time in the history of the game—that's what was making the cash registers sing. Did labor relations create McGwire and Sosa's fabled chase? Did labor relations ask Barry Bonds to hit 73 home runs in one season? I don't think so.

The other thing that really irked me was the shamelessness with which Mitchell betrayed his bias toward the Red Sox, for whom he was a director when the investigation began. Anyone who follows baseball knows that the biggest rivalry in the game is between the New York Yankees and the Boston Red Sox. I found it interesting that Mitchell named about twenty past and present Yankees, including some of the biggest players—such as Roger Clemens, Andy Pettitte, Jason Giambi, Gary Sheffield, David Justice, Chuck Knoblauch, Kevin Brown, and me (I played for the Yankees during their 2000 Championship season), but that few names appeared from the Red Sox roster. Mo Vaughn? He hadn't been on the Sox since '98. And Eric Gagne played only half a season with them before signing with the Brewers for the 2008 season—and that was a scant four days before the report was released. Hmmm. Interesting timing.

Why the discrepancy? Does the Big Apple really have that many more juicers than Beantown? I seriously doubt it. I played on both teams, and when I said four out of five players were juicing, I meant *across the board*. And Beantown was no exception. This exhaustive report, which was conducted *independently* and *with no bias whatsoever,* would have us believe that the New York Yankees were a bunch of juicers, while the Red Sox were almost as clean as a whistle. Again, I don't think so.

What's more, there were no current Marlins in the report. Zero. A few former players, but nothing to worry about. Mitchell served on their board of directors. I'm not saying that means anything, of course, but I just thought I should point it out. Feel free to draw your own conclusions.

For his part, Mitchell said, "You will not find any evidence of bias, of special treatment of the Red Sox or anyone else, because there is none." Oh, well, at least that eliminates any doubt. Thanks.

Overall, I'd have to say I found the report disappointing, and that's a gross understatement. They had spent tens of millions of dollars to tell us something most of us already knew, and the fact that it was organized into nice, tidy sections didn't mean a hell of a lot to me. The whole exercise seemed designed more to make it *look* as if MLB was doing something about the problem, instead of actually doing something.

I especially liked the part where they talked about the danger of using steroids and other performance-enhancing drugs. They are dangerous, but every idiot knows that by now. And kids who didn't know it needed to learn it pronto (and I didn't think too many kids were going to be reading the Mitchell Report). What wasn't known or perhaps understood as clearly as it should be, and what Mitchell and his team missed, was *why* the use of steroids had become so widespread. And I'm going to tell you why: the players weren't taking steroids because they enjoyed them, or because it was so much fun; they were taking them to keep up with the competition. Without steroids, many of them felt, not unjustifiably, that they would lose their edge. And without that edge, they felt, with great certainty, that they would lose their jobs.

The formula was pretty simple: Take steroids, have job security. Don't take steroids, try your luck in the minors. You'd be hard-pressed to find a guy who didn't reach the top, or close to it, without steroids, except for maybe one: Derek Jeter. I believe Jeter was clean. He is a perfect example of a great player who didn't use the edge to turn himself into a superhuman player, and of the price one pays for doing so. In a culture that expects you to do anything and *everything* to become the best, the guy who doesn't cave gets left behind by his peers. Take a closer look at Jeter; measure him against every other superstar shortstop in his class. Track the stats. Jeter built his way into the Hall of Fame, without steroids, only to be outdistanced by a number of guys who were probably getting juiced.

If I learned anything from the Mitchell Report—aside from the fact that it supposedly cost north of $20 million to produce—it related to those long-ago rumors about that FBI investigation. According to the Mitchell Report, all those rumors were dead-on, including the one about the Feds talking to MLB about the scope of the problem, which they described as "widespread," and the one about MLB's refusal to do anything about it.

Still, when all was said and done, I was most perturbed that so many obvious names had been left out of the report. What had happened to Ivan "Pudge" Rodriguez and Juan Gonzalez, for example? I didn't have anything against those guys, but I'd pumped steroids into their butts, and I'd written about it in my book. Why weren't their names in the report? Ivan had started out at about 170 pounds, went all the way up to 240, and quickly dropped forty pounds in the months following the publication of my book. Coincidence? I don't think so. I suspect that Pudge—or, more accurately, the Player Formerly Known as Pudge—had gone on the Fear of Being Found Out Diet.

Other names never made the Mitchell Report, and I couldn't understand it. When I wrote *Juiced*, I didn't name every single player who had done steroids, or whom I suspected of having done them, partly because I figured I had enough names, and partly for reasons I will get to in due course. But the Mitchell Report wasn't a book. This was a hugely expensive report to the commissioner of baseball, you'd think they would have done their best to leave no stone unturned. I was curious to understand their reasons for leaving out the names of known users and even of suspected users. It wouldn't have required much effort.Surely they read my book. And I talked to two of their guys out in Santa Ana. Yet those names weren't in the report.

I got an A-plus on my lie-detector test. I think the Mitchell Report deserves a disappointing D, or maybe even a D-minus. Half of it wasn't there and the other half was only half-true. So maybe the report wasn't total fiction, but it was badly flawed, and I myself could have told them that they got many of their facts wrong. The business about Clemens being at my party, for example—that was fiction.

How could they ignore such blatant evidence and still call their report comprehensive?

6

DEAL WITH THE DEVIL

In 1984, shortly after I lost my mother, I began taking steroids, and for much of the rest of my professional career, until my forced retirement in 2002, I didn't stop for long, just long enough time to let my body readjust. I have often said that I got into steroids because I promised my mother, on her deathbed, that I intended to become the best baseball player in the world. And I have also said, more than once, that I did it to win the approval of my father, a tough but well-meaning man who was never satisfied with anything that I, or my twin brother, Ozzie, ever accomplished. He was a perfectionist, and he wanted his sons to be perfect, but he set the bar a little high. We could never live up those expectations, though I think I came close in the 1988 season, with my 40-40 and Most Valuable Player Award.

Those reasons are true enough, but at the end of the

day, I've realized that I made the decision myself, and I'm not trying to avoid any blame or make any excuses. I decided to start using steroids.

I was twenty at the time, still grieving for my mother, and I was confused about my life. I was already a pretty good baseball player, but I was on the scrawny side, and I lacked confidence. Some of that lack of confidence stemmed from the constant beating my ego took over the years, at my father's hands, but in some ways those emotional beatings are also what drove me to succeed.

And I really *wanted* to succeed. Not just because I'd made a promise to my mother but because I was looking for direction. I was looking for a purpose. I was looking for a path that would make my life make sense.

By that time, of course, I had already decided that I was going to become a professional baseball player. Or maybe baseball had decided for me. I'm not sure. All I know is that I liked hitting, and that I was actually pretty good at it.

But not good enough.

As luck would have it—maybe good luck, maybe bad— I ran into a friend from high school, a weight lifter, at precisely the perfect time. Maybe the stars lined up right. Or wrong. I don't know. All I know is that I was looking to bulk up, that I didn't feel that I was strong enough, and that the gym alone didn't seem to be doing it for me.

"I'm working out hard, harder than I've ever worked out in my life, but I'm not seeing the results I should be seeing," I said.

"I know exactly what you need," my friend said. "Steroids."

Over the next couple of weeks, he taught me everything he knew about steroids. He was smart and articulate, so I paid close attention.

Anabolic steroids are synthetic hormones, derived from testosterone, and are designed to build bulk. That's what they do. They put on muscle. They make you bigger. Doctors use them to promote tissue growth.

In addition to being smart, my friend was buff and perfectly healthy, and by that time he'd already been doing steroids for a few years. So it was an easy decision. I'd try them. I'd take my chances.

Looking back from my vantage point of more than two decades, I wonder if this is the way that kind of stuff always works. Somebody does a line of coke in front of you, and his head doesn't explode, so you figure it's safe. Or somebody drops a tab of acid, and he doesn't start speaking in tongues, so you figure you'll give it a try. I've never tried any recreational drugs, but I imagine the first time runs down that same type of path.

With the decision made, it was time to get started. On the big day, I went back to my friend's house, where he got a syringe ready, told me to brace myself, and stuck the needle in my butt. It hurt for a second, but I didn't make a peep. "It's going to take a few moments to get into your system," he said. "Relax."

I tried to relax, but it was tough. As I said earlier, I half-expected to grow a third eye, or *worse*, but nothing happened. We then went directly to the gym, to work out, and I didn't feel a damn thing. I started to get really worried.

"Nothing's happing," I said.

He laughed. "Jose, man—I thought you were paying attention. This shit ain't instant. Give it time, get through the cycle."

He sure was right about that. It wasn't anything like instant. If anything, I felt a little *weaker*, but that's probably because I was so nervous, still wondering whether something was going to go terribly wrong. I couldn't afford to slow down or end up with some type of injury that would keep me off the baseball field for even a day.

After the workout, my friend was still laughing. He could see the wheels turning nonstop in my head. "You are the most impatient guy I know," he said.

"I can't help it," I said. "I want to get good, and I want to do it fast."

"It's not magic, you know? It's not like you can sit on the couch in front of the TV and expect your muscles to develop on their own."

"Who's sitting in front of the TV? I'm working out."

"That's good. Because if you're looking for real results, if you really want to kick ass in baseball, you're going to have to work harder than ever in the gym."

For an entire month, nothing happened. I worked out harder than ever, a man possessed, but there wasn't any discernible change. Finally, one day, I guess the shit must have kicked in, because I noticed a genuine difference. I had more of a pump, more endurance, and the burn actually felt good. I noticed I could do more and felt much better.

And that's how it began.

From that day on, I was hooked. The shit was working. And I liked the way it made me feel.

Back then, steroids were pretty much in their infancy, and nobody seemed to know that much about them, but I decided to become an expert on the topic. So I dug around for information. In the muscle magazines, in fitness journals, at the library, gathering as much information as I could get my hands on. Nowadays, you can punch the word *steroid* into a search engine and about 20 million articles will pop up. I know, because I've looked at a few of them, and most of them are kind of scary.

You're going to get cancer and liver tumors. Your heart's going to clog up. Your testicles will shrink. Your sperm count will drop to next to nothing. Guys can also end up growing breasts, which is pretty sad. Instead of rippling abs, bulging biceps, and ballooning quads, you end up with tits. Me with tits? Now *that's* scary.

Back then there was no Internet, however, and I did my research the old-fashioned way. I worked at it.

When it came to training, I did it the old-fashioned way, too. They didn't have those bogus fat-burning machines, or equally bogus machines that used mild electric jolts to build muscle while you slept. I was completely committed to making myself the most powerful hitter in baseball, and I worked out like crazy. I also paid attention to everything else, from what I ate and when, to how much I slept, to what parts of my body weren't getting the attention they needed. I even studied every supplement and vitamin that sounded as if it might fit my needs. In short, I turned into one of those guys who treated his body as a temple, and I did it for good reason: I wanted to kick ass in baseball.

Before long, my career took off, and it just kept going. And year after year, I learned more and more about steroids. I was my own guinea pig, a guinea pig with pecs and power and serious definition.

Was I worried about the effects? No, not really. And it wasn't as if I were wearing blinders. I heard the wild stories—the quiet guy next door, for example, gripped suddenly by 'roid rage. "He was the nicest man in the world. Never hurt a fly. Then suddenly, for no reason at all, he went after her with a claw hammer."

And more recently, of course, tragedies in the world of wrestling. It got people thinking about steroids. And about sports. And about the shit people were doing to succeed.

Still, I didn't know anyone who had ever attacked another person with a claw hammer. And I had no personal connection to any of those wrestlers. To me, these were stories on the evening news. They were real, certainly, and some of them were sad as hell, but even the experts couldn't explain them. Steroids affected different people in different ways, they said. Maybe other drugs were involved. Maybe it had nothing to do with steroids. And maybe, for some people, steroids awoke the monster within. Nobody really knew. There certainly wasn't a scientific consensus that steroids caused these problems.

But one person would always come forth with the big revelation: "He was addicted to steroids. He couldn't live without them."

Addicted to steroids? Well, I'll give you this much: I believe there *is* an addictive component to steroids, but I don't believe it's physical. I believe it's purely psychological. And it's easy enough to understand: the steroids are really working for you. You're feeling strong, looking good. And before long you get to a point where you're a little afraid to give them up. "I can't give them up," the guy thinks. "I'll lose my edge if I stop juicing." And you know what? He's probably right. He *will* lose his edge. But steroids aren't addictive in the traditional sense. Your body doesn't crave steroids. Your mind isn't screaming for more. You just want them because they make you feel so right.

Still, even if that "addictive" component was a problem, it was the only problem I had.

I know my ex-wife used to say that I was catatonic at times, but that's just me. I'm the shy, quiet type. An introvert. Sometimes I get lost inside my head. That's all that was. I was never very social (and she complained about that, too).

Even at the gym, where little groups of guys hung out together, talking about steroids and supplements and chemical cocktails for hours on end, I wasn't interested. I did my own research. And I wasn't one of them. I kept to myself. I'm not a joiner. Never was. Steroids didn't make you antisocial. And they didn't make you social, either. Not me, anyway.

On the baseball field, however, with my fellow players, I was much more receptive. We had something in common. We were baseball players. And every last one of us wanted to be a better player. So when they came to me, I was happy to share everything I knew. I was even happy to stick needles in their asses. And the more I learned about the stuff, the more eager I was to spread the cheer.

These were grown men, after all. Looking for an edge. And we were part of the same show, baseball, the greatest show on earth.

Kids, though, that's a different story—and from what I'm reading lately, a little worrisome. Twelve- and thirteen-year-olds were getting into the shit, and that's downright dangerous. Anyone who isn't well past puberty shouldn't go anywhere near the stuff. You're messing with hormones, and steroids can knock your system out of balance with ugly results. Unless, of course, you like guys with tits and girls with beards.

But seriously: Not to preach, but parents need to be vigilant. If your kid is an athlete, for example, struggling to make it to the front of the pack, and he gets there a little too quickly—well, take a closer look. The signs are obvious. I think parents often just turn a blind eye to the problem. Their kids are messing with stuff they shouldn't be, but because they're getting better on the field, the parents pretend not to notice. You have to notice. You have to make sure they aren't creating big problems for later in life. And if the kid is looking impressively bulked up, *too* impressively, *too* fast, that's definitely worth thinking about.

What can you do about it? Take him or her to the family doctor for a routine checkup, then sit back and wait for the results of the blood test. You'll have your answer within forty-eight hours.

The stuff is out there, people. And it's tempting. Kids today want more and they want it faster and they want it now.

I know *I* was like that. Hungry. Impatient. And it's worse for kids today. Everything is available with the click of a mouse. Instant gratification has been taken to a whole new level. And sure, it makes everything more convenient, but it's got its dangers. You start expecting everything to happen *right now*, and steroids sound as if they might just deliver. It doesn't work that way, though. And kids need to know that. Parents should learn about the dangers and the side effects and have a heart-to-heart with their kids. Be vigilant, because it's just too easy for underage athletes to jump right in.

Still, it *is* a shortcut. And even back then I knew it was a shortcut. And after my friend walked me through Steroids 101, I knew I had found what I was looking for. I had to work for the results, of course, harder than I'd ever worked before, but I liked what I was seeing, and that made it well worth the effort. Before long, the hard work was paying off on the baseball field.

Had I made a deal with the devil? Well, yes. Probably. And all I can say in my defense is that I was trying to be the best version of me that I could be.

And, yeah, I know what you're thinking: in my first book, I said that steroids were here to stay, and I said I *guaranteed* it. In some ways, I guess I was endorsing them. I said I thought steroids were the future, and that for the intelligent user—the user who opted for professional supervision—they would probably never be a problem. I even predicted that the informed use of steroids would someday become the norm, and that I was actually looking forward to that day.

But I've changed my mind. It's been three years since I wrote *Juiced*, and *I've* changed, and I no longer believe everything I believed back then. To me, that's progress. Life is about forward movement, and I'm moving forward. I'm still the same guy, but an older, wiser, and—hopefully—slightly improved version of my former self.

So, yes, I admit it: there are things I might change about my past. If I had it to do over again, I might not do steroids. Steroids cost me two marriages. Not because of any aberrant, steroid-related behavior, but because so much of my life was focused on the stuff. Steroids became the center of my existence, and my never-ending experiments—my battle to make myself the strongest, toughest guinea pig on the planet—pretty much took over. I was doing it for baseball, sure, but I was pursuing baseball with such single-mindedness that there wasn't much left over for normal life. So maybe it wasn't steroids that cost me my marriages, but my single-mindedness about baseball, which obviously included steroids. I guess the same could be said about all of it. My devotion to baseball cost me a normal life and all the things a normal life provides.

Maybe that's what it takes to succeed in this crazy

world—that kind of drive. Maybe that's what it takes to be the best. But life also calls for balance, and I had zero balance. I was a baseball machine with one overriding thought in my head: to get better-faster-stronger. And it's *all* I cared about. When I wasn't on the field, practicing or playing, I was *thinking* about practicing or playing, and about the perfect steroid cocktail that would take me places no baseball player had ever before been.

And I got there. But guess what? Everything I accomplished in baseball—the records, the huge amounts of money—that's all gone, too. Just like my two marriages.

That said, I'm not going to tell anyone how to live his or her life. If you're an adult—and I stress *adult*—and you are set on experimenting with steroids, I'm not going to stop you. But at least be smart about it. Work with professionals. Don't be buying stuff from a guy who stashes it in the trunk of a beat-to-hell Datsun. Or from that painfully pumped-up dude who's always in the gym, no matter what time of day you show up. Talk to someone you can trust, such as your doctor. Steroids are a serious business and should be taken seriously.

One final thought on the topic: People often ask me if I think performance-enhancing drugs messed up the game, and I'll be honest with you—I don't believe they did. They made the game entertaining, and the fans got their money's worth (and then some). The average person works a nine-to-five job and struggles to make ends meet, and if he's going to go out to the ball game—parking, seats, hot dogs, popcorn, beer, licensed merchandise, and all the rest of it—the show's got to be worth his while. If nothing else, the Steroid Era made it worthwhile for the fans. That's my opinion, anyway. The thrill of watching a too big guy with a too big head knocking a 600-foot homer out of the park, who doesn't enjoy that? I know I did. I enjoyed watching my fellow players, and I enjoyed batting those moon shots into the stratosphere. After all, I'm an entertainer. That's what I was supposed to be doing—entertaining—and I'd like to think I succeeded from time to time.

But sometimes too much of a good thing is too much of a good thing. Sometimes enough is enough. At some point, admittedly, the whole steroid thing started to get a little crazy. And while it's good to push the envelope, maybe we pushed a little too hard. Some big freaks were out there, maybe too big. At some point the guys were thinking, "How much bigger can I get? And how long can my body take this?" The truth is, nobody knows. Guys just kept getting bigger and bigger, and records were being broken almost every day—to the point where they stopped meaning anything.

So, if you're asking me, and even if you're not asking me, I say we bring the Steroid Era to a close. Put away those damn syringes. Get back to the basics. Move forward. And Major League Baseball needs to put effective testing procedures in place. If no one is on steroids, if no one has an edge, then we'll get back to that level playing field.

The single biggest issue now relates to all the records that were set, what they mean, and what we're going to do about them.

As a result of the scandal, a lot of people are still questioning the integrity of the game, and they're questioning its credibility. But many of those people also seem to want to have it both ways. Are McGwire and Sosa cheats and liars, or did they save baseball during their fabled chase?

And where do we draw the line, anyway?

I mean, it's not like I want to defend those guys—not *all* of them anyway—but are we not going to make room in the Hall of Fame for Roger Clemens? Barry Bonds? Mark McGwire? (And by the way, Mac, haven't you heard: *There's no crying in baseball.*)

You can't penalize all these guys, and certainly not retroactively. When you think about it, "I'm not here to talk about the past" has kind of a nice ring to it.

And really, aren't we overdoing it?

It's true that anabolic steroids bulk you up and make you stronger. Maybe it's even true, as I've read, that they improve visual-spatial function, which means you might even be getting a tiny edge—a fraction of a fraction of a second—when the pitch comes barreling toward you.

But when you add it up, what are you adding exactly? A 1 percent edge? Two percent? What about the raw skills these guys were born with and worked so hard to develop? Do those count for nothing? Wasn't Barry Bonds one of the greatest players of his time even before he bulked up?

Steroids don't make you great, people. They give you a leg up, a *nice* leg up, but that's about it. Steroids will not take a guy like Danny DeVito and turn him into Barry Bonds.

So, yeah, let's move on. People will look back at this as

the Steroid Era, and they'll understand the amazing records in the context of the era.

And you know something else? From where I stand, it *was* a level playing field. We're not talking about a handful of juicers; we're talking about the vast majority of the players on the field: 80 percent or *more*.

They were doing it for themselves, sure—to hold on to that edge, to keep their jobs. But the results were also great for the fans. They got a great show. A fantastic and exciting time to be a baseball fan and follow the sport.

You know what they say: *Everyone digs the long ball.*

And it's true. The fans love the long ball, but they love the rest of the game, too. You have to believe that. The game can be just as much fun on a lower, level playing field. Players are still going to hit hard, even if the numbers are smaller. What's wrong with 30 homers in a single season?

Ask yourself this, do you want to watch superheroes, or are you okay with regular guys playing the game to the best of their abilities?

And, hell, it's not like baseball has always been squeaky-clean. The game has a rich tradition of cheating: gambling, spitballs, corked bats, and worse. The game has been around for 130 years, and we've seen it all: the Juiced Ball Era. The Corked Bat Era. The Spitball Era. The Pitcher's Era. The Power-Hitter's Era.

This will go into the books as the Steroid Era. It's as simple as that.

There is nothing constant about baseball. The game is always changing and evolving, and not necessarily for the better. Instead of trying to fix the past, which is unfixable, we should learn to live with it.

Stop crying already. How many times do I have to tell you:

There's no crying in baseball.

7

VINDICATED

When I look back on the weeks and months following the publication of my first book, I now find the whole thing sort of amusing. Back then, though, I wasn't laughing.

Palmeiro wagging his finger during the hearings, denying he'd ever done steroids. McGwire getting all weepy, saying he wasn't there to talk about the past but about the future (not that he had one). Curt Schilling not really knowing *what* he was talking about. Giambi, who had the balls to call me "delusional." Even Tony La Russa, my old manager from Oakland, went out of his way to attack me, describing my book as "a healthy case of envy and jealousy." Every one of those guys has been proven wrong, but ask me if a single one of them has so much as acknowledged it.

And the reporters, my God, what a bunch of clowns! I

was "easily dismissed." I had "no credibility." I was "lying through my teeth." It was easier to attack the messenger, I guess, than to listen to the actual message.

Then there was the never-ending barrage of denials from the biggest juicers in the business: "I never knowingly did steroids, Congressman. I was just strolling back to my locker, calm as you please, when two big guys grabbed me and pinned me to the floor, and a third guy, a *really* big guy, lifted up my towel and poked me in the ass with a needle. I have no idea what it was, but I'll tell you this: It was absolutely horrible! And that same thing happened every day for six weeks! I couldn't get away from those guys! And, no, I don't know why I was suddenly hitting more home runs than ever."

As for the story with Clemens, it kept getting weirder and weirder. On January 6 of this year, 2008, as I was putting the finishing touches on my new book, Clemens appeared on *60 Minutes* to defend himself against the charges, most of which had been leveled by Brian McNamee, his former trainer. "Never happened," he told Mike Wallace, insisting, yet again, that he had never taken steroids. "And if, if, if I have these needles and these steroids and all these drugs, what, where did I get them? Where is the person out there [who] gave them to me? Please, please come forward."

On the other hand, he did admit that he was hitting the painkillers big-time. "I was eating Vioxx like it was Skittles," he said. He sounded like the Clemens I'd always admired, willing to do anything to help his team win.

My favorite part of the interview, though, was when he

talked about the *amount* of stuff McNamee claimed he was doing. "I should have a third ear coming out of my forehead," he said. "I should be pulling tractors with my teeth."

Well, I did that amount of stuff and more, and I still only have the two ears I was born with. As for the tractor part, yes, some days I felt I could pull one with my teeth. But what was the point? I had better things to do with my teeth.

A couple of days after Clemens's television appearance, he sued McNamee, calling his statements "absolutely false and defamatory," and not long after—surprise, surprise—Roger's lawyers reached me on the phone to talk about McNamee and about the Mitchell Report.

I told them about Roger not being at my party, which I had already discussed with him, and they asked if I would be willing to sign a sworn statement to that effect.

"Sure," I said. "Whatever Roger needs."

A couple of days later, the lawyers called again, and they arranged to fly me to Houston to put the affidavit together. When I got there, Roger picked me up at the airport, and we drove to the attorneys' office. Roger was pretty upset, understandably, and he repeatedly denied the allegations against him, and by the time we got to the lawyers' office I began to wonder whether I'd been wrong about him all along. After all, a person can change his mind. And if and when he does, he should have the courage to admit it.

I spent many hours with Roger and with his lawyers—there were three or four of them in the room, which was a little overwhelming—and they crafted a document based on our on-going talks. At one point, they asked me if it was okay to include the following: "I have never had a conversation with Clemens in which he expressed any interest in using steroids or human growth hormone. Clemens has never asked me to give him steroids or human growth hormone, and I have never seen Clemens use, possess, or ask for steroids or human growth hormone.

"I have played on three teams with Roger Clemens and I have no reason to believe that he has ever used steroids, human growth hormone, or any other performance-enhancing drugs."

The first part I had no problem with, but the last sentence was troubling—at least initially. I had always suspected that Roger had been juicing, but suddenly I was no longer sure. I really didn't know what to do, but I knew I needed to be truthful, as I had been from the start—about everything. I could certainly attest to the fact that I didn't have firsthand knowledge of his steroid use, but did I honestly think the guy was clean?

Technically, I didn't have a *single specific* reason to believe that Roger had used steroids, but based on his behavior, and based especially on his performance, I had always felt he was using. But now, Jesus—I was very confused. I was sitting there with Roger and a bunch of lawyers, and I didn't know what to think. I kept asking myself, *Do I have one compelling reason to believe he used steroids? One single specific reason that convinces me, beyond the shadow of a doubt, that Roger was juicing?* The answer was no. No, I did not. And the more time I spent in that room, with the lawyers and with Roger, the more I came to believe that I'd been wrong about him.

So I signed the affidavit.

If it sounds confusing, that's because it *was* confusing. I had an abrupt change of heart, yes, and I wish I could explain it better. I felt bad for Roger, sure, and I let myself get sucked into his drama. And maybe that's exactly what Roger and his lawyers wanted. I honestly can't say. All I can say is that suddenly Roger had me believing he had never juiced.

The sad part is that on February 13 I watched him go head to head with Brian McNamee, during the ongoing congressional hearings, and old Roger didn't come off too good. Maybe I'd been right the first time. Maybe he had been juicing. And maybe I'd been wrong to change my mind. But in my heart, during my visit to Houston, I came to believe the guy. If I hadn't believed him, I never would have signed that affidavit. And if I'm wrong about Roger, and he *was* juicing, I'm pretty sure we'll know before this book even hits the stands.

But I'm getting ahead of myself. About two weeks after Clemens appeared on *60 Minutes*, steroids were in the news again. The FBI said it was trying to determine whether Miguel Tejada, the American League MVP in 2002, had lied to federal authorities when he denied taking performance-enhancing drugs. "Everyone knows me," Tejada told reporters. "The only thing I know is playing baseball and playing tough."

Two days after that, NFL player Dana Stubblefield was actually charged with lying during the early part of the

BALCO investigation, the same investigation that brought down Olympic sprinter Marion Jones.

Man! They were falling left and right.

In my case, given everything I went through, things have turned out amazingly well. But I knew that all along. I'm an optimist. I'm a believer. I believed that the truth would ultimately prevail.

When I returned from my first book tour, exhausted and still reeling a little from the viciousness of the attacks, one of my old friends came by to talk me into playing in a Sunday baseball league. "It's a good bunch of guys," he said. "You'll like them. And some of them are pretty decent players. Come on out. Have a little fun. You'll enjoy getting the old baseball *juices* flowing." Yeah, yeah. Very funny.

So the following Sunday, I went out and met the guys. They really were a good group. They were welcoming, fawned a little (without overdoing it), and I was offered a choice of position on the field. "Well, if you don't mind," I said, "I think I'd like to pitch."

"Then pitching it is!"

It had been a long time since I'd pitched, and it was a disaster. I couldn't find the strike zone, and I must have walked thirty guys. But nobody complained. They were forgiving and supportive, and I got better as the day went on.

A couple of former minor leaguers were on the team, and the other guys were mostly serious amateurs—weekend warriors who were not completely without talent. As a result, the games were more challenging than I'd expected them to be. More fun, too. I really started getting into it.

I ended up making a whole new group of friends, which

was also a good feeling. I'd been pretty well abandoned by my other friends, and these guys weren't passing judgment. None of them had a beef with me. It was just a bunch of guys with a common interest in getting together and playing competitive ball. It felt so good to be "home" again. I love the baseball field.

In the weeks ahead, I pitched some—not quite as disastrously as in that first game, thank God—and I played third base, which I had played back in high school, on the varsity team. I began to look forward to the games. I felt energized and happy. And when I was on the field, the rest of the world simply didn't exist.

We played all over the San Fernando Valley, just outside L.A. We had sponsors, and uniforms, and a good crowd always turned out to watch. We were competitive, and we were serious, but mostly it was about having fun.

I think it's safe to say that I was the best hitter on the team. We used aluminum bats, and the balls are what we call flat-restricted. The core of the ball is softer so it doesn't travel as far as a "normal" baseball.

One day, a local reporter came out to watch the game. He wanted to do a friendly article about me—"Jose Canseco Playing in a Sunday League," that kind of thing—and he picked the right day to come. I ended up crushing one of those flat-restricted balls, and it went 480 feet. That was a record for that field, and it gave the reporter something to write about. He led with that hit.

The guys in the league were thrilled. We were getting a little press; I was putting them on the map. There was a picture of us in the paper, doing our Sunday thing. It wasn't exactly the *New York Times,* but it was enough for us. I'm sure a lot of those guys framed that article and hung it on their walls.

"If you can't make it to the major leagues," one of them told me, "bring the major leagues to you."

I guess that's pretty much what they had done.

Most of the guys also got around to reading my book, but they seemed to be taking their time about it. For a while, I wondered if they had only invested in *one* book and were passing it around, because every Sunday a different player would approach me to discuss it. It was a real pleasure to find myself talking to people who were reading *Juiced* for what it was, and who understood why I had written it and what I had hoped to accomplish. We were finally talking about content, not about my credibility.

For a while, throughout this period, I sometimes wondered what had happened to my old friends, and at times I half-expected to hear from them. But it didn't happen. Clearly, I was no longer part of that world. To them, I was a pariah, and they'd always see what I'd done as a betrayal. They would never understand or acknowledge that I'd done it for love of the game. But that was okay, too. I had new friends, and a whole new life. I enjoyed the new chapter in my life, determined not to look back.

Then in early June 2006, I got a call from some guy in San Diego. He represented the San Diego Surf Dawgs, part of the Golden Baseball League, and he got right to the point: "We saw an article about your Sunday league in the newspaper. We were wondering how you'd feel about playing for us."

"Sounds interesting," I said. "What did you have in mind?"

Within a week, we had a contract. I had to add only one clause—permission to skip an occasional game if it conflicted with the Sunday league, which I wasn't about to abandon—and they had no problem with that. The money was incidental, of course—it always is at that level—but I wasn't doing it for the money. I thought it would be fun to get back into the game on a professional level, even if that level was a far cry from the majors.

I signed the contract, then drove down to San Diego for my first game. A bunch of reporters were already there—the league must have tipped them off—but they were unusually nice. I'd been pretty much redeemed by my performance in the congressional hearings and by the many steroid-related articles that followed, not to mention several books on the subject, so they treated me pretty well.

They asked a few questions, and I answered them.

"How does it feel to be playing again?"

"I don't know. Ask me after the game."

"Isn't this a little out of your league?"

"I love baseball."

"How did your book do?"

"Well, it was number one in the *New York Times*, and I don't think it gets much higher than that."

"Do you still talk to your old friends?"

"What friends?"

"Seriously."

"No. I have hardly any connection to that part of my

life anymore, but I'm not complaining. I have great new friends, and my life is good."

"How much is this league paying you?"

"Enough to pay my gardener."

"Seriously."

"I would do it for free," I said. "But don't tell them that."

"What position are you going to play?"

"Whatever they want me to play, but I like to pitch. And I like third base because I played third base in high school."

"What have you heard about the Mitchell Report?"

"Not much."

"Has Mitchell contacted you?"

"No, but I spoke to a couple of his clowns a few months back."

"What did you tell them?"

"You'll have to wait for the report."

One of the newspaper guys asked me if I didn't think I was getting a little long in the tooth for baseball, but he did it good-naturedly. And the guy had a point. At forty-two, I was a good fifteen or sixteen years older than my team-mates, and when they first saw me, they looked a little shell-shocked. I wasn't old enough for them to call me Pa or anything, but it was close. Still, I don't see myself as old. And I certainly don't *feel* old. And I still had it. At the end of that first game, I was voted onto the All-Star team, and that game was only three days away.

When I returned for the All-Star Game, which we played at Nettleton Stadium, in Chico, the place was completely sold-out. I was told it was the first time that anything like that had happened in the league's entire history. The owners were happy, obviously, the players were happy, and I was happy. I'd been asked to join the league because someone thought it might spike attendance, and that someone had been right. I took the time to sign a few autographs and to pose for pictures with the fans, and it felt just like the old days. I was playing ball again.

Before the All-Star Game got under way, we did the Home Run Derby. I was playing against sixteen of the best hitters in the league, and no one expected me to win. Except me. I am not going to try to be modest here. Some real talent was out there that day, and I knew I was in for a challenge. But I locked in and the ball kept jumping off my bat, one home run after another, and I won.

I got a standing ovation from the fans. I don't suppose I need to tell you how that felt.

Just being out there, playing, in front of a capacity crowd—well, it brought back all sorts of old feelings. It wasn't a major league stadium, and we didn't have major league lights or fancy major league cameras or giant major league monitors, but everything about it felt right. It was baseball. It was home.

And who needed all that fancy shit? I didn't need to look up at the monitor to watch myself doing whatever it was I'd just done.

I was there because I loved baseball. I loved my new team. I hadn't played pro ball in five years, but there I was, doing what I'd always loved doing.

We lost the game 7–6, and I'm sorry to say I didn't help

much. I was pitching in the fourth inning, showing off my knuckleball, and I gave away four runs, letting the other guys take the lead.

When it was over, the fans poured onto the field, and I spent the next hour signing more autographs, posing for more pictures, and even signing copies of my book for the people who'd had the foresight to bring them. I'm just happy that nobody said anything about my uninspired performance in the fourth inning.

I remember, in particular, one father and his son. They waited until the crowd had thinned before approaching me. The kid was shaking with excitement. "He's just nervous about meeting you," the father explained. "You're one of his heroes."

That felt great. The kid was twelve, maybe thirteen. He knew baseball. It's not like the steroid scandal passed him by. "Thank you for thinking of me as a hero," I told him. And I meant it, too. From the bottom of my heart. Here was a kid who'd been born after my 40-40 season, after my MVP, but I still did stuff, on and off the field, to earn his respect. How could you ask for more than that?

On the drive home, I kept thinking about how much fun I'd had, and how absolutely everything about the day had been a blast. I was happy to be playing ball again. I loved staring down the pitcher, waiting for my shot. And really, there's nothing like crunching that ball into the stands. Nothing. Every time you connect like that you remember, all over again, what it is you love about the game. Not that I needed reminding. I've loved the game since I first picked up a bat.

There was only one thing I couldn't handle, and that was the drive to San Diego from my home in Los Angeles. Without traffic, it should only take a hair over two hours, but there was always traffic, and I felt like a commuter, trapped in my car for six hours a day. Yes, a *day*. They were serious about the game. We played every day. But I couldn't take the drive, so I asked them if they could possibly trade me to another team, and I mentioned the Long Beach Armada, which was a lot closer to home.

The Long Beach team was just as much fun as the guys in San Diego, and just as happy to have me. They were just as young, too, and equally shell-shocked by my "advanced" age. Here again, local reporters showed up to watch my debut, and they asked similar questions.

"Are you happy you wrote the book?"

"Very."

"Do you miss baseball?"

"Every day. That's why I'm here."

"How do you feel?"

"Sore and happy, which is how a ballplayer should feel."

It was a great season, and it was hard work. I was in pretty good shape because I have never stopped working out, but playing baseball is different from working out. In baseball you use muscles that you forgot you had, and when you wake them up, they whine and complain. Some days I went home and soaked in a hot tub for hours. I'd had plenty of injuries in my career, and they have a way of creeping up on you, more so if you begin to tease those sleeping muscles. In fact, some days my body was no more than a collection of aches and pains, but I loved the game so much that the aches and pains felt good—a reminder of my major league days, perhaps—and I powered through.

I was sore for the entire season, until the last couple of weeks, when my body stopped complaining. By then, of course, it was time to hang up the cleats. It was kind of funny. I felt the way I usually felt at the end of spring training. You've been sore forever, but you're finally catching your stride, and you're ready to go to the show. Only in this case it was over. I was ready, but it was over, and I was going home.

To me, the season had a lot of great games, and one truly memorable game. In Long Beach, the field has this odd shape, and nobody had ever been able to crush a ball over the right-center fence. I didn't believe it couldn't be done, and I kept trying. I got the ball over every other fence, and over the stands, but I just couldn't manage the right-center fence.

"Never happen," the other players said. "Can't be done."

Finally, on that memorable night, I really crushed the ball, and in my heart I just knew I had done it. Everyone turned to look, waiting for a miracle, but it fell short. I guess I will not be rewriting the history of that field.

During the season, I also played a couple of games with my Sunday league, per that clause in my contract. We didn't win the title, but second place was respectable enough. And nobody complained. The guys were as competitive as any players I knew, but more than anything else they were about a good time. There was no crying in the clubhouse that night.

I did not go back for another season with the Golden Baseball League. They asked me to return, but I decided against it. I had loved it, and I had appreciated the chance to get back into the game, but my time away from the game had given me new perspective on life, and on the need for balance. I needed to accomplish other things. Plus it was time to move on. Best of all, this time around I was leaving the game of baseball on my own terms, which was satisfying indeed. And, hell, I still had my Sunday league. Maybe all I really needed at that point was one or two games a week.

By this time, my book had long since disappeared from the front pages. I'd still get calls from time to time, someone looking for a comment, or for a short interview, and I tried to be nicer to the press than they'd been to me. Occasionally, some reporter would call from Holland or somewhere, asking for a story, and I'd try to humor him, but half the time he didn't know what I was talking about. Try explaining baseball to a guy whose English you can't even understand. When I got off the phone, I wondered why he was even writing about baseball. Did they have baseball in Holland? I knew they had cheese, and windmills, but I didn't think they had baseball.

My social life revolved around my daughter, my friends, and a few business associates. I worked out every day, played poker, made appearances for worthy causes, and even decided to try my luck with acting. I think I got the bug after that stint on *The Surreal Life,* although I know better than to call that *acting.* I began taking lessons with Howard Fine, a well-respected local acting coach, and I hoped that with hard work and a lot of luck he might be able to turn me into a half-decent actor. If he didn't, though, I wasn't worried. I was having fun with it. Plus, some good-looking women were in the class, and I enjoy looking at attractive women.

As I pursued this new career, I ran around Hollywood, taking meetings. Everyone was extremely nice, but nothing much happened. People were eager to meet me, and some of them were amazed at my size, and at the shape I was in. A typical comment was "I knew you were a big guy, but I didn't know how big." Many of them wanted to talk about the book, and about how we might turn it into a movie. One executive compared it to *The Insider*. A guy blows the whistle on powerful people—MLB, in my case—and they set out to destroy him.

"I like that," I said.

"So do I," he said. "Let me discuss it with the group."

I never heard back from him. And despite all the meetings, and all the kind words, nothing much ever happened. A friend in the business finally explained it to me. He said that people in Hollywood tell you how much they love you, and how much they love your ideas, because they don't like confrontation, and because they think it's nice to be nice. "I hate that," I said. "I'd rather they were honest with me."

"That's the way it works," he said. "Somebody once described Hollywood as the only place in the world where you could die of encouragement."

The only place in the world where you could die of encouragement? That was funny. I liked that.

Still, you know me—good old single-minded me. Nothing was going to stop me. I kept going to meetings and listening to various "takes" on my story. It was definitely about a little guy who took on the system—in this case, a six-foot-four, 240-pound little guy—and it was great because it had that whole David-versus-Goliath thing. But now the problem was that nobody knew how the story turned out.

"The ending hasn't been written yet," one executive said.

"I thought that's what writers were for," I said.

"Well, yes, but this is a true story. I think we're all waiting for the Mitchell Report."

Another executive said, "This is a story about the man who saved baseball."

I loved him for that, and I thought he had a great *take*, but I never heard from him again.

I'm still making the rounds, though. I'm not a guy who gives up easily. I even put the pitching aside for a while and found myself auditioning for a part that would have put me on-screen with Nicole Kidman. I know, I know. I sound like every other wannabe actor in Hollywood, but I'm not making this up. The producers liked my size, and they liked my looks, and they seemed to think I was perfect for the part: a bodyguard who gets involved with Nicole. They called me back a couple of times and even taped my audition, but it didn't work out. Maybe they thought I didn't have enough experience (which would be about right, since I had zero experience). Or maybe they didn't like my reading. Or maybe they decided not to make the movie after all, or to not make it with *me*. Was I disappointed when I didn't hear back from them? Of course I was! Hugely so. But so what? I would keep trying. That's who I am. And the reason I am the way I am is that I know the secret of life. And the secret of life is this: You fall down. You get up. That's it. It doesn't get any simpler than that.

When the Mitchell Report was finally released, producers started calling again, anxious to develop a screenplay, but now we had a new problem: the Writers Guild of America was on strike. People loved my story, but we couldn't get it written because the writers were on strike.

So I kept auditioning. And I kept hearing the same thing, always delivered with a pleasant smile: "Thanks—that was great—we'll call you." Or not.

It wasn't all bad, though. Thanks to the Mitchell Report, I was back in the papers.

In December 2007, Jon Friedman of *MarketWatch* had this to say: "The media's convenient scourge of the Mitchell Report, which named about ninety current and former baseball players as steroids abusers, was none other than Jose Canseco. His sin was emerging as a seer and the voice of reason in the crisis, while fans should ask why much of the sports media were asleep at the switch and failed to uncover the wrongdoing.

"I suspect that plenty of sports reporters view Canseco as the enemy, even more so than some of the accused players. Why? Simple. They are angry because Canseco scooped them in baseball's biggest scandal ever—yes, it's weightier than the dark time when eight Chicago White

Sox players took money from gamblers and conspired to throw the World Series in 1919, forever becoming immortalized as the Black Sox."

The emerging truth also seemed to be helping some of the players come clean. That same month, Shane Monahan told ESPN that he had used steroids when he was with the Seattle Mariners, back in 1998 and 1999. He was a fringe player who was having a hard time sticking with the majors, and he had found one way to do it. "I've been in minor league and major league clubhouses," he said. "I know the pressures and what goes on. Like I told my dad, it is coming from the perspective of a guy who had to fight for everything he got in the big leagues.

"I saw what kind of money it is going to get you. I had great minor league seasons, but I wanted to stay in the big leagues. I know my teammates and I know guys on other teams are doing it, and they're hitting home runs left and right. And I'm sitting there going, 'Alright, well, what am I going to do?' "

I loved what this guy had to say. I loved that honesty. I had been honest in my first book, which had been the goal. And he was echoing the exact pressures I was describing. The money, that so many other players were getting the edge steroids provided. Players had to jump on steroids to compete with all the other players on the drugs.

So, now, almost three years after the publication of my book, I felt I wanted to tell the rest of the story, write the ending those producers had been looking for. I wanted to talk about everything that had happened to me since *Juiced* was first published, and I began to put out some feelers.

There was immediate interest, and of course, someone leaked it to the press.

John Donovan of *Sports Illustrated* had this to say: "Well, if Canseco's first book and the fallout from it proved anything, it's that you ignore him and what he has to say at your own peril. Much of what he related in *Juiced* was more accurate than anyone in baseball would like to admit. . . . In many circles, Canseco is now recognized as the man who first exposed the true depth and breadth of baseball's Steroid Era. He has become the opposite of what many considered him to be. He is now . . . credible."

That's right, I'm credible. And in addition to sharing with you everything that has happened to me in the past three years, I am going to share with you the names of a few players who never made it into my first book. And they are not just any players, either. One of them is even bigger than Roger Clemens.

Now, I know what's going through your mind. You're thinking, "If he had these names all along, why did he leave them out of his first book?" Well, I had *two* good reasons. The first is that I felt I had enough names. The book was never about naming names—it was an exposé of Major League Baseball—but I couldn't have sold it without names. The publishers said they needed names, and I saw their point. So I named names—I named just as many players as I thought I needed to name. I had also named Clemens, of course, because he was a big name and an important player, and I knew that his inclusion in the book would make people sit up and take note. After all, this was a guy who until recently was a lock for the Hall of Fame. In fact, he was well on his way to becoming the first unanimous selection to the hall *ever*. How could anyone deny his stats, the awards he'd racked up over the years, and the undeniable presence he had over his career? Clemens was a widely respected, much loved, decent, all-American guy, almost a *symbol* of everything that was good—or was once good—about baseball. So, yes, I figured that having Clemens in the book would get people's attention. And I'm sure I was right. But he ended up on the cutting-room floor for reasons I can still only guess at. Maybe he was too well liked, so that even the lawyers who were vetting the book were disinclined to link him to the scandal. Or maybe it was simpler than that. As I look back on it now, I realize that I had a much more personal connection to every other player I named in the book, not in terms of friendship, but in terms of steroid use. In every case, I was either personally involved in administering steroids, or I had been responsible for putting them in touch with a supplier. And in every one of those cases, I had also been around to witness the physical changes.

Even then I couldn't say that about Clemens, though, and I never did. I had my suspicions, and Clemens even made little jokes about Deca flying out of my veins, but that didn't mean he was a user. The lawyers might have felt it was too risky to include Clemens, and they must have based that on three reasons: One, I had not seen him do steroids. Two, he had never approached me about using steroids. And three, I had never steered him toward anyone who could supply him with steroids. All I had were conversations with him about steroids, and my general suspicions. It wasn't enough.

I had plenty of names that made it into the book, of course, including two players—Wilson Alvarez and Dave Martinez—who were clearly not "confused" about what they'd been doing. We discussed the steroids, they made the decision to use the drugs, and I personally injected them. Still, somehow, strangely enough, neither Alvarez nor Martinez made it into the Mitchell Report, and all I can say to that is, "Nice work, Senator."

I left two names out of my own book, but I had legitimate reasons. (*Two* reasons, as I said. You've heard the first; I'll get to the second in a moment.) The first name was Magglio "Maggs" Ordonez, a certified superstar. I met Maggs in 2001, when I was with the White Sox. He played with the White Sox from 1997 to 2004, then went off to join the Detroit Tigers. He signed a five-year, $75 million contract with the Tigers, the largest deal in that team's history. Maggs is a right fielder and a three-time Silver Slugger, known for his quick, short stroke. In 2007, arguably the best season of his career, he was the American League Batting Champion, batting an eye-popping .363.

Maggs became a friend. He approached me and was up-front about what he wanted, and what he wanted was for me to tell him everything I knew about steroids. He wasn't one of those guys who said, "Skip the details. Just jab that needle in my ass and make me strong." No, he was a smart guy who was going to base his final decision on solid information. He wanted all the details. Pros, cons, side effects—everything. And I took my time. I answered every question.

"How much you spending on the shit a month?" he asked me.

"Oh, I don't know, it varies. Maybe eight to ten thousand."

"And you get it from a good guy?"

"Different guys," I said. "But don't pay with personal checks."

"That makes sense."

Maggs wanted to know more: the good, the bad, the ugly.

"Then your balls disappear," I said.

"What?!"

I laughed. "Well, they don't disappear exactly, but they definitely get smaller."

"I don't know if I like that."

"Your dick stays the same."

"Oh," he said. "That's good."

"You've got to watch your diet, though. Some guys think you can eat crap if you do steroids, and you'll still develop muscle, but that's only partly true. You should eat healthy and exercise more than ever."

"Okay," he said. "What about going crazy? I hear some guys go crazy."

"Do I look crazy?"

"A little," he said, but he was smiling.

"I'm telling you, you're going to be fine. Steroids are the future. One day, everyone will be on them. They'll be like part of our morning routine."

"I have one more question."

"What?"

"Am I going to get too big?"

"No." I laughed.

"Why are you laughing?"

"Because everybody asks that question."

When it was all said and done, when Maggs had the information he needed, he told me he was in. A few days later, we went into a back room in the clubhouse, and I jabbed a needle into his butt.

"Ow," he said. "That hurt."

"You'll get used to it," I said.

"What happens now?"

I laughed.

"What are you laughing about this time?"

"I'm laughing because everyone always says that, too. They think they're going to grow a third eye, or that their head will turn into a balloon or something. And they always think they're supposed to feel something right away."

"I know, I know—you told me."

"That's right, I did," I said. "Don't expect anything to happen for four to six weeks."

If you're having trouble believing me, go back and look at the lie-detector tests.

Did you inject Magglio Ordonez with growth hormone or steroids?

Jose: Yes.

And remember, according to the experts, there was *zero chance* of deception on my part. It's no longer just my word against everyone else's. I've got the lie-detector tests to help me refute the knee-jerk reactions of people who just want to lash back at me and accuse me of lying.

I injected Maggs a couple more times, with steroids and with human growth hormone, and then he was on his own. I don't know if he learned how to do it himself or if he had someone do it for him.

A few weeks into it, not surprisingly, the guy started to change. He was bulking up, modestly but solidly, and was feeling good about it. Maggs had found the edge he'd been looking for. The steroid shortcut was working for him, and working in a big way.

If he crushed one into the stands, I'd see this happy look on his face as he took off around the bases: *Man, this shit is good*. And when he got back to the dugout, it was always the same thing: "I'm feeling good, Jose. *Me siento bien*."

Flash forward to 2005. My book came out. I didn't name Maggs in my book. I didn't name him because I had enough names, and because somehow, in a small way, I must have felt a small connection to Maggs, must have felt we were almost friends. So, yeah—I played favorites.

Suddenly everyone was calling me a rat and a liar. I toughed it out and laughed it off and pretended it didn't bother me. But, it *did* bother me. And I had some pretty lousy moments. During one such moment, I wanted to speak to someone who would understand what I was going through, someone whom I played with who understood Major League Baseball and understood how steroids played such a big part. I reached out to Maggs, and to his agent, Scott Boras. I left messages. I said I would like Maggs to call me back. He never did. And it pissed me off. He didn't want anything to do with me. I had told the truth, and Maggs knew I had told the truth, and here he was, just like everyone else, treating me like a pariah. Ignoring me and writing me off.

Am I naming him now to get back at him? No, not at all. I am naming him because he has, right or wrong, come to represent everything that bothers me about all the assholes who came to me when they needed something, but who weren't there when I needed them. I didn't think Maggs should offer himself up to Congress. I wasn't asking him to out himself. I didn't want him or anyone else to step forward and back me up by speaking the truth: "Jose Canseco has taken an awful lot of shit, but in fact he is telling the whole, unbelievable truth. I know this because I have seen much of what he has seen, with my own eyes, because I am a user of steroids myself, and in fact, Jose jabbed me in the ass with a needle full of steroids." No. I wasn't asking for that. I was just reaching out to an old friend in a time of need, just looking to talk.

In a sense, Maggs was worse than the guys who lied to Congress. I was asking for so little from him, and he gave me nothing.

Then the story got even weirder. According to a January 24 article in the *New York Times,* I had offered to keep

Ordonez "clear" in this new book, *Vindicated*, if he invested in a documentary film I was trying to get off the ground. I didn't understand what the word *clear* meant, or why the newspaper wasn't naming its mysterious source, "a person with knowledge of the situation." If I was really trying to shake Ordonez down, why didn't they just say so? Was it perhaps because Ordonez himself admitted, in the same article, that we had never spoken and that I had never approached him for money?

The *Times* went on to say that "referrals were made from Major League Baseball to the FBI," and that they were somehow connected to this alleged shakedown, but no one had the balls to be quoted by name, and even Ordonez refused to talk about it. "I didn't want to press charges against [Canseco]," he said. "I don't want any problems." Really? The bigger problem was that I had never even spoken to the guy, not about my book and not about a documentary. I had reached out to him, as I said, in a time of need, but he never returned my call, so I *couldn't* have offered to keep him out of my book. That seemed pretty significant to me, but the two *New York Times* reporters who filed the story, Michael S. Schmidt and Duff Wilson, didn't seem to have a problem with it.

I was further surprised to discover that Maggs's agent, the mighty Scott Boras, had also filed a complaint with the FBI, saying that I had called his office and spoken to one of his associates, offering to keep Maggs "clear" if he invested in my nonexistent film. The associate was never named, however, and even Boras admitted that he had never talked to me personally, not about Maggs and not about my book. And there was that word again, *clear.* What exactly did it mean?

As I thought about all of this, it occurred to me that Major League Baseball was up to its old tricks. They were going to do everything in their power to discredit me even before *Vindicated* hit the stands. I found that sort of amusing. Hadn't that backfired on them the last time around? Didn't these idiots learn anything from their mistakes?

If someone had something to say, why didn't he man up and let the newspaper quote him by name? And if Ordonez really thought he had a case against me—despite the fact that we never even spoke—why didn't he press charges? Hell, if someone tried to shake me down, I know I'd do everything in my power to go after the son of a bitch. Makes you wonder why he was holding back, especially since it was clear he'd been told that I was going to be naming him in my book.

The more I thought about the article in the *Times,* the more steamed I got. Then I realized I could do something about it. On Friday, January 25, only days after that bullshit story appeared, I went back to see John Grogan, the man who had administered one of my previous lie-detector tests, and he put me through the paces. I told him I wanted to address each specific allegation, and that's exactly what we did.

Did you ever at any time tell Magglio Ordonez that if he invested in a movie project of yours he would be "clear" in your next book?

178

Jose: No.

Did you have anyone call Magglio Ordonez to tell him that if he invested in a movie project of yours he would be "clear" in your next book?

Jose: No.

Did you ever personally speak to Magglio Ordonez relating to a five-million-dollar investment?

Jose: No.

Have you ever spoken to Magglio Ordonez about any matter in the last six years?

Jose: No.

Have you ever spoken to Scott Boras about any matter in the last six years?

Jose: No.

Did you ever speak with anyone at Scott Boras's office regarding a five-million-dollar movie project?

Jose: No.

Did you ever speak to anyone at Scott Boras's office about whether you were going to name Magglio Ordonez in your next book?

Jose: No.

Have you or anyone on your behalf ever tried to extort money from Magglio Ordonez for any reason whatsoever?

Jose: No.

Once again, I passed with flying colors. *Absolutely no deception indicated*. I'd like to see Maggs and Scott Boras sit through similar tests. I wonder how they'd do.

Anyway, that's the story on Maggs. Maggs Ordonez, who last year was runner-up for the American League's MVP crown, a man I personally injected with steroids.

Now we get to other guy: A-Rod. That's right, Alex Rodriguez, who has already made baseball history and who isn't done breaking records. It was A-Rod, in fact, who outplayed Maggs to become the American League's Most Valuable Player in 2007, so I think it's safe to say that we're talking about two pretty impressive names.

Now, as you may recall, I told you I had *two* reasons for not naming these guys. The second reason applies only to A-Rod, and I'm going to share it with you now: the reason I didn't include A-Rod in my first book is that I hated the bastard. That's right. I hated him too much. For personal reasons that I'm going to explain. And I never made a secret of the fact that I hated him. I hated him so much, in fact, that—if I'd included him in my first book, people would have questioned my motives. So I didn't name him. It was that simple. I didn't want my negative feelings for A-Rod to muddy the waters.

For those of you who don't follow the sport, A-Rod is the biggest thing in baseball right now. At age thirty-two, he has had more home runs, more runs batted in, more runs scored, and more base hits than all the other greatest players did when they were his age. More RBIs than Hank Aaron; more home runs than Barry Bonds; more runs scored than Rickey Henderson; and more hits than Pete Rose. Those guys are legends for excelling at one or two stats, but A-Rod is kicking ass in *all* of them. There is no doubt, barring some freak accident, that A-Rod will become the youngest player in the history of the game to reach every magical benchmark ahead of him. Hell, he already has 518 home runs and more than 1,500 RBIs. And everyone knows he's well on his way to breaking the all-time Major League Baseball home-run record of 762, set by Barry Bonds in 2007. And, of course, he is being richly rewarded for it. Not too long ago, A-Rod signed a ten-year, $252 million contract with the Rangers, the richest contract in sports history. And more recently, even before that contract had expired, he signed a new, bigger one, with the New York Yankees, with the potential for a $30 million bonus if he actually surpasses that 762-home-run record.

That $252 million figure wasn't arbitrary, by the way. Up until that point, the largest professional sports contract belonged to Kevin Garnett, who had signed with the Minnesota Timberwolves, of the NBA, for $126 million. By asking for, and getting, exactly double that amount, A-Rod was beating his chest and telling the world, "I am twice as good, and worth twice as much, as any other athlete on the planet. And don't you forget it."

I think you get the picture.

Anyway, let me take you back to the latter half of the 1990s. A-Rod was a kid, but a talented kid. Skinny, too. I don't think the guy weighed much more than 200 pounds.

I was living in Florida at the time, in a house that had a five-thousand-square-foot gym, and A-Rod came over one day, to check out the property and to work out with me. I thought he was gifted ballplayer, and I told him so.

"You are going to be the next guy to do forty-forty," I said.

"No way," he said.

"Trust me, man. You could become the greatest player in baseball history."

The first day he was there, my then wife, Jessica, joined us in the gym, and A-Rod's eyes bugged right out of his head. For the rest of the workout, he was pretty much drooling, and when she left the gym, he was still in mild shock. "Man," he said. "Your wife is the most beautiful woman I've ever seen!"

"Yeah," I said. "She's not bad."

For a brief period—this was during the off-season— A-Rod was coming by pretty frequently, partly to work out, and partly to stare at my wife. When he wasn't ogling my wife, though, he'd be looking at me—not in the same way, of course—and you could see he was thinking real hard. One day, he decided he wasn't going to keep his thoughts to himself.

"So," he said. "The 'roids: Do they fuck you up?"

"Do I look like I'm fucked up?"

And that was the end of that conversation.

The next couple of times he was over, Jessica wasn't

around, and I could see he was pretty disappointed. "Where is she?" he asked. I guess he just couldn't hold back.

"I don't know," I said. "Out somewhere, spending my hard-earned money."

"Man, she is the most beautiful woman I've ever seen in my life."

What the hell was A-Rod's problem? There were plenty of women around, readily available and wildly aggressive. I would go into clubs and restaurants with my wife on my arm, and they would literally push her aside. "Oh, Jose, you are even more handsome in person!"

Even the married girls did it, with their husbands watching from nearby, getting steamed. "I'm free Monday to Friday, while he's at work. Regular business hours." Talk about shameless!

On the road it was even worse. The girls would be hanging out in front of the hotel, hoping to catch a glimpse of us on our way in, or they'd be waiting in the lobby near the elevators. "Well, hello! My prayers have been answered! God is *good*."

And yeah, I know—we were in the middle of the off-season, but that shouldn't have been a problem. A-Rod could have walked into any bar in town and had his pick of any woman in the place—along with all of her little friends, come to think of it, because half of them would be reaching for their cell phones the minute they spotted him: "You've gotta come quick, Sheila! You're never going to believe who just walked into the bar!"

But hey, maybe that didn't happen to A-Rod. Or maybe

it did, but he only wanted my wife. Pissed me off. The guy sounded like a love-struck adolescent. "Jose, man, that Jessica, she must be the most beautiful woman in the world."

"Yeah," I said. "I heard you the first eight times."

"Well, she is."

"Why don't you concentrate on your workout?"

"I'm concentrating! I'm concentrating!"

"Not hard enough."

He looked at me. I could see him checking out the definition; the way my veins popped with every curl.

"Man, you are kicking ass," he said. "That stuff is unreal."

"Yes, it is," I said.

"And you've never had a problem with it?"

"Never."

He then began calling Jessica on her cell phone. Supposedly, he was calling her about a friend of hers, this hot girl he'd bumped into at the house, after one of our workouts, though of course I had my suspicions. I'm not a jealous man, but I could see that A-Rod, a bachelor at that time, was jonesing for my wife.

Right around this time, I ran into a trainer I knew from Canada, from my old days with the Toronto Blue Jays. I'll call him Max because I'm going to leave it to him if he wants to go public. He was down visiting in Florida, and he was looking to make a little money and maybe try to move down to the Miami area permanently. This trainer was a fan of steroids, and he had connections with local suppliers—we often traded information on where we got our stuff—and he knew almost as much about the subject as I did. He asked me if I knew anyone who could use his services, and I told him I'd ask around.

The very next time Alex came over, he asked me, point-blank, where *one* would go to get steroids if *one* wanted them. He was a cautious, cagey guy, Alex. He didn't say, "I want to buy steroids. Can you point me in the right direction?" Or, more accurately, as far as I'm concerned, he *did* say it, but not in those exact words.

Now, maybe you don't see it that way, but if someone comes to me and says, "Hey, Jose, do you know where one can buy farm-fresh eggs?" I figure that person is looking to buy farm-fresh eggs. And I could see that A-Rod was interested in his farm-fresh eggs. Our conversations about steroids had piqued his interest and he was intent on pursuing the subject.

"Yeah," I said. "I know where *one* would go if *one* wanted to buy steroids." I looked right at him. He actually seemed a little nervous. "If you want, I can introduce you to some guys. In fact, I know a guy with plenty of access, and he also happens to be a very good trainer."

"That would be good," A-Rod said. "I'd like to meet this guy. Is this a guy you trust?"

"Completely."

"Great."

That night, I called Max and told him that Alex Rodriguez was interested in meeting him.

"To train?" Max asked.

"Yup."

"Man, that's great! What about the other stuff? He interested?"

"He sure as hell seems to be, but that's between you and Alex, and I'm staying out of it."

"I just want to make sure I can talk to him about it."

"Hey," I said. "We're all big boys. We all know what we're talking about."

"Okay. Maybe I won't say anything right away. Maybe I'll let him bring it up."

"I think that's smart."

The next day, I called A-Rod. I told him I had spoken to the trainer, and we made arrangements to meet at my place the following day. When they showed up, I made the introductions. *A-Rod, this is your trainer (and supplier), Max, this is your client, A-Rod.*

Take another look at that lie-detector test:

Did Alex Rodriguez ever approach you about acquiring steroids or human growth hormones?

Jose: Yes.

Thereafter, did you introduce Alex Rodriguez to someone who you knew had supplied other athletes with steroids or human growth hormones?

Jose: Yes.

Believe me now?

The next day, Max called to thank me. He said A-Rod

had signed on. I didn't ask for specifics. I didn't ask if A-Rod had signed on to get trained, or to get shit from this guy. That wasn't my business.

After that, I didn't see too much of Alex. For one thing, he was off with his new trainer, training at a regular facility, not in my private gym. For another, a few days after I'd made those introductions, while I was sitting with Jessica by the pool, her cell phone rang. I was closer to it, and I saw A-Rod's number on the screen. She answered it, and they talked for about ten seconds, then she got off the phone.

"Why is that guy calling you all the time?" I said.

"He's not calling all the time, and he's not calling for me," she said. "He's looking for Amy."

"Doesn't feel right. I go out of my way to help the guy, to be nice to him, and this is what he does behind my back."

"He's not doing anything behind your back. The guy is harmless."

Harmless. Sure.

As I was writing this book, and I thought back to this whole mess, I suddenly figured something out. As you can see from everything I've told you, I *introduced Alex to a known supplier of steroids*. In other words, if I had decided to include him in my first book, he should have passed the hurdles the publisher seemed to invoke, unlike Clemens. I was not personally involved with administering the drugs, no, but I *had* put him in touch with a supplier. I just thought I needed to make that point.

Anyway, I didn't see A-Rod for many weeks—not until

the New Year, as I recall—and when I did, it was completely by accident. I was with Jessica at the time, driving past some Miami club, and we saw him standing near a valet stand, waiting for his car. Jessica saw him first, actually, and she waved and called his name, but I guess he didn't hear her. I turned to look at him as we drove past. "He was looking pretty buff," I said.

"I didn't notice," she said.

I'm confident it was the 'roids. I believed it then, and I believe it now. I've been down this road too many times with too many guys. I know my shit, and I know the way it works. I may not have seen him do the deed, but I set the whole thing up for him, just like he wanted. I saw the changes in his body in a short time. Hell, if you ask me, I did everything but inject the guy myself.

Not long after, I caught him calling my wife on her cell phone, *again,* and she and I got into a fight. I screamed at her that A-Rod was a known cheater, that he had no morals, and that she should open her eyes. "Don't you get it?" I shouted. "The guy just wants to fuck you!"

I felt bad later for screaming at her. She hadn't done anything wrong.

After that, I didn't see A-Rod for many years, not until long after my marriage had fallen apart, when I ran into him at a club in Los Angeles, and I got right to the point: "Why did you try to fuck my wife, Alex?"

"Fuck you, man," he said. "I never tried to fuck's anyone's wife. I'm a man's man!"

What the hell did that even mean? *A man's man?* The guy was a known cheater. If you don't believe me on that point, try your luck with Google. Put in *Alex Rodriguez* and *infidelity* and you'll get about fifty thousand hits.

"Stray-Rod," they call him.

Or, "Alex Rodriguez is a Cheating Ass."

Or my own personal favorite, A-Rod "Likes the She-Male, Muscular Type."

Did I mention that I don't like the son of a bitch? Well, I don't.

But that's not why I'm telling you this. I'm telling you this because he is a hypocrite and a liar. And because he has no morals. And I don't like people with no morals.

But, hey, Alex puts asses in the seats. And he's rich. And he's powerful.

And he's not a bad ballplayer, with or without the steroids.

So you've got to respect him, right?

And you know what's really strange? Many years later, when I got tossed into that Miami jail cell on that bullshit steroid charge, I met an inmate who turned out to be an informant. "You have two very powerful enemies," he told me.

"Only two?" I said.

"Two I know of."

"Who are they?"

"One is Major League Baseball."

"I knew that, I've been living with that for years," I said.

"The other is Alex Rodriguez."

"Really? Alex Rodriguez. That asshole tried to fuck my wife."

189

"I don't know what he tried or didn't try with your wife, but I know he hates you. He's been telling people he'd like to see you in jail for the rest of your life."

"What good will that do him? If it's about my wife, my wife isn't my wife anymore. He should call her. Maybe *his* wife won't mind."

"Maybe he already has."

"Well, I wish him lots of luck," I said.

But I didn't mean it. I thought the guy was an asshole then, and I haven't changed my mind.

So A-Rod, if you're reading this book, and if I'm not getting through to you, let's get clear on one thing: I hate your fucking guts.

8

THE TIME LINE

I often think of myself as the guy who brought Major League Baseball into what is now commonly known as the Steroid Era. Turns out I didn't do it alone, but, hey—I did my part and then some. With that in mind, I thought it would be interesting to take a look at how we got to where we got, and, just as important, at least to me, where I fit into the equation.

So without further ado, I'll get started:

JULY 2, 1964 *Jose Canseco is born in Havana, Cuba.* As someone who changed the game of baseball twice, first by introducing steroids, then by exposing them, I think this is an important date. (My twin brother, Ozzie, was also born around this time, but this is my book.)

1982 *The Oakland A's draft Jose Canseco in the fifteenth round.* Baseball had been my life for a long time, and suddenly my dreams were coming true. From that day on, I was a bona fide professional baseball player. Ask me how that felt.

1984 *Jose Canseco is introduced to steroids.* After my mother passed away, God rest her soul, a friend introduced me to steroids. I had promised my mother that I would become the best baseball player in the world, and I was determined to keep that promise. I jumped on steroids just like I jumped on fitness and baseball practice and eating right and not partying—like I jumped on everything that could help me reach my goal and fulfill my promise.

SEPTEMBER 2, 1985 *Jose Canseco makes his major league debut.* After three years in the minors, I played my first MLB game against the Baltimore Orioles at the Coliseum. I only had one at bat and never made it on base, but I was finally in the show.

1986 *Jose Canseco wins American League Rookie of the Year.* Thirty-three homers and 117 RBIs, not bad for a rookie season, right? I was making my mark, and I had no intention of stopping.

NOVEMBER 18, 1988 *Anti-Drug Abuse Act of 1988.* This act made it illegal for people to have or to sell anabolic steroids without a doctor's permission. Translation: I had to be more careful.

1988 *Jose Canseco named American League Most Valuable Player.* With the first 40-40 season in MLB history (42 home runs, 40 stolen bases), 124 RBIs, and a batting average over .300, the voters had no trouble deciding that I deserved the award. I thought so, too—I led the league in home runs, RBIs, and slugging percentage. We also made it to the World Series that year, but lost to the Los Angeles Dodgers.

OCTOBER 28, 1989 *Oakland A's win the World Series.* After losing the previous year, getting my ring this time around meant even more to me. Winning the World Series is everything you might imagine, and then some. No, I take it back. You can't imagine it. It's an amazing, indescribable experience, plus your name is in the baseball history books forever.

OCTOBER 5, 1990 *1990 Anabolic Steroid Control Act.* This was basically more of the same. Steroids were still illegal, but with more things in place now to catch and punish users. Did it work when it came to baseball players? Ask yourself this: how many athletes have gone to jail for steroid use? (I'm aware that Marion Jones was sentenced to six months, but that was for *lying* about her steroid use, not for using steroids.)

JUNE 7, 1991 *Major League Baseball tried getting in on the antidrug action.* Commissioner Fay Vincent sent a memo to every MLB team to let them all know that steroids were on the list of banned substances. Clearly, MLB knew it had a problem on its hands, but even so, it didn't bother with any kind of testing program.

MAY 7, 1992 *Operation Equine.* An FBI sting operation discovers that steroid use is widespread in professional baseball, other sports, and even in the Olympics. They secretly share their findings with MLB, but nothing much happens.

1992 *Jose Canseco is traded to the Texas Rangers.* Part of me was sad to leave Oakland, admittedly, but before long

I'd hooked up with some good people. Rafael Palmeiro and Juan Gonzalez were friendly from day one, and that made the transition a lot easier.

1994   *Baseball strike.* A big black eye for the game. The fans saw the owners as fat-cat billionaires who only cared about money, and the players as spoiled brats who were looking for a bigger piece of the pie.

JULY 1995   *The cat is out of the bag.* Padres general manager Randy Smith told the *Los Angeles Times,* "We all know there's steroid use, and it's definitely becoming more prevalent." Yet again, nobody did anything. Why? MLB was trying to recover from the strike. They didn't want to muddy the waters.

1995–96   *Jose Canseco plays for the Boston Red Sox.* I had two pretty good years there, hitting 24 and 28 home runs, respectively, with more than 80 RBIs in each season.

1997   *Jose Canseco goes back to the A's for a season.* I was reunited with some names and faces from the past, including former "Bash Brother" Mark McGwire (who partway through the season was traded to St. Louis). My stats dipped a little, but I was still a solid player.

AUGUST 22, 1998   *Mark McGwire and andro.* Right in the middle of the home-run race with Sosa, The Chase that "saved baseball," androstenedione was found in Mark McGwire's locker. McGwire admitted that he used it, but noted, rightfully, that it was not illegal in baseball. He then went on to break a thirty-seven-year-old record by *nine* home runs. I think Mark hid that andro in plain sight for a reason: he wanted to deflect potential questions about steroids. (Sorry, Mark, I couldn't resist talking about the past.)

1998   *Canseco has his best season in years.* While Big Mac and Slammin' Sammy were getting all the attention, I put together one hell of a season for the Toronto Blue Jays. I had 46 home runs and 107 RBIs. It felt great.

JUNE 30, 2000   *Steroids are found in a MLB player's car.* A batboy got pulled over while driving a car that belonged to big-leaguer Manny Alexander. The cops found steroids and syringes in the car, but didn't charge either the batboy or Manny.

APRIL 2001   *The minor leaguers start getting tested.* I guess this was a step forward, but it still seemed like they were saying, "Okay, we're going to start testing everyone . . . except anyone who's in the majors." A first offense led to a fifteen-game suspension; a fifth and you were banned for life. Sure seemed like they were giving you all the opportunities in the world.

OCTOBER 6, 2001   *Jose Canseco plays his final major league game.* I finished my career with the Chicago White Sox, after spending some time with the Devil Rays (twice) and the Yankees.

JUNE 18, 2002   *The government gets involved.* John McCain, getting ready to run for president, takes the least controversial stance in political history: illegal drugs should be illegal. Way to go, John. McCain and his fellow politicos tell Selig and Donald Fehr that they need to make sure there's some testing that works better than the lousy plan now in place. (Or words to that effect.)

AUGUST 30, 2002   *MLB begins testing.* In an effort to determine the scope of the steroid problem, MLB gets into "survey testing."

The good news was, the results were going to be confidential, and the penalties were basically nonexistent. Players would not be suspended, and they wouldn't be turned over to the police.

FEBRUARY 17, 2003 *Orioles pitcher Steve Bechler dies.* Steve was twenty-three when he collapsed on the field just before the start of the season. The official cause was listed as heat exhaustion, but an autopsy found ephedra in his system. Major League Baseball immediately put ephedra on the list of banned substances—but only in the minor leagues. Major league players, minor leaguers on forty-man major league rosters, and players who have been optioned to the minors are unaffected by this policy because they are members of the MLB Players Association, and the MLBPA has yet to take a stance on ephedra. They will only agree to test for substances that are banned by the U.S. government, which is still weighing its options.

OCTOBER 29, 2003 *More banned substances.* The Food and Drug Administration banned THG (tetrahydrogestrinone), a synthetic "designer" steroid. MLB, clearly unable to act on its own without a kick in the ass, bans it the next day. Smart thinking, guys!

NOVEMBER 13, 2003   *Survey-test results announced.* A total of 1,438 players were tested anonymously for performance-enhancing drugs, and we were expected to believe that only 5 to 7 percent had tested positive. Still, MLB put a mandatory testing plan in order, but it was a plan without teeth. If a player got caught, he'd have to talk to medical professionals and be tested again later. If he got caught again . . . well, we'll figure something out.

DECEMBER 2003   *Players testify before a grand jury.* Barry Bonds, Jason Giambi, Gary Sheffield, and others were called to testify in front of a grand jury as a result of their connection to the Bay Area Laboratory Co-Operative (BALCO). You all know what happened when some of the testimony was leaked: Giambi admitted to using some illegal performance-enhancing drugs, Bonds admitted he "unknowingly" used some performance-enhancing drugs, etc. Hmmm.

MARCH 2004 *Politicians want more of the spotlight.* McCain talked tougher about steroids and sports than about anything else, or so it seemed. "Your failure to commit to addressing this issue straight on and immediately will motivate this committee to search for legislative remedies," he told MLB. Are you scared yet?

APRIL 12, 2004 *FDA bans the manufacture and sale of ephedra. Citing the link between ephedra and more than 150 deaths,* this legislation marks the first ban of a dietary supplement by the federal government.

MAY 11, 2004 *The World Anti-Doping Agency gets involved.* In a move that made more sense than almost anything else they'd done up to that point, MLB and the players' union decided to let the WADA conduct the drug tests. Obviously MLB was doing a lousy job on its own, so they turned to the professionals. It was actually a shock to see MLB doing something intelligent.

OCTOBER 22, 2004 *More politicians step up to the plate.* President Bush signed the Anabolic Steroid Control Act of 2004. MLB had agreed to ban whatever Congress banned, so suddenly a lot of stuff was on the list.

JANUARY 13, 2005   *The drug program gets tougher.* Major leaguers are told that they will be suspended for ten days for a first offense. The idea of counseling a player for a first offense seemed a little ineffective.

FEBRUARY 14, 2005   Juiced *is published! My first book bursts onto the scene and causes a genuine shitstorm.* I told it like it was, and no one believed anything I had to say. The guys I wrote about knew I'd written the truth—McGwire, Palmeiro, Giambi, Juan Gonzalez, etc.—but they and everyone else called me a scumbag and a liar and said I was out to make a quick buck.

MARCH 5, 2005   *Selig announces test results.* If you believe good old Bud, only 1 to 2 percent of players tested positive for steroids or other performance-enhancing drugs. That's twelve people. If you believe that, I guess you believe I never went near the stuff, either. I saw more than twelve juicers in the same clubhouse, but why believe me?

MARCH 8, 2005   *Players get subpoenaed for a congressional hearing.* The House Government Reform Committee wanted to know more about steroids in baseball. Why? Because *Juiced* told them there was a huge problem, and they thought it was high time they looked into it.

MARCH 17, 2005   *The hearings get under way.* A lot of the characters in my book were there, and some of them put on a really good show. Not very convincing, though. Unlike some people, I didn't have to hide behind the Fifth Amendment. I had told the truth in my book, and I told the truth again that day.

APRIL 3, 2005   *First suspension.* Alex Sanchez of the Tampa Bay Devil Rays became the first major league player to fail a drug test after the new program was in place. Per the new rules, he was immediately suspended for ten days.

APRIL 4, 2005   *Minor leaguers get failing grades.* Just one day later, we were told that thirty-eight minor leaguers had tested positive for steroids. More suspensions followed.

MAY 18, 2005   *Commissioners get their day in court.* The top dogs in major sports met with the subcommittee and were subjected to more stern talk from the politicians. They wanted tougher policies, which were put into effect a week later. It was proposed that a player be suspended for two years for a first steroid offense and banned for *life* for a second.

AUGUST 1, 2005 *Palmeiro tests positive for steroids.* Just a few months after his adamant, finger-wagging denial, Rafi eats crow. You know my theories on this one.

NOVEMBER 15, 2005 *The penalties get harsher.* A fifty-game suspension for a first offense, a hundred games for two, and a third strike puts you out of the game forever.

MARCH 23, 2006 Game of Shadows *is released.* Everyone had been waiting for the hammer to come down on Barry Bonds, who had been destroyed by public scrutiny and whispers, and this book, by Mark Fainaru-Wada and Lance Williams, tells the whole, unvarnished story.

JUNE 7, 2006 *Jason Grimsley busted.* The Arizona pitcher is busted by the Feds, and he names names. Way to have your personal shipments mailed to your own home, pal.

JUNE 2006 *More players come clean.* On the heels of Grimsley's bust, David Segui and Paxton Crawford, among others, admitted they had used either HGH or steroids. Good move. In my book, it's better to confess than to get caught.

JUNE 29, 2006 *Jose Canseco signs a deal with the Golden Baseball League.* I'm back playing, briefly, with the San Diego Surf Dawgs, then I'm traded to the Long Beach Armada so I could be closer to home. Ask me who won the Home Run Derby.

OCTOBER 1, 2006 *Big leak, big names.* Allegations abound. Clemens, Pettitte, Tejada. How far does this go? About as far as, or farther than, Jose Canseco told you it went.

DECEMBER 13, 2007 *The Mitchell Report is released.* It names eighty-eight Major League Baseball players alleged to have used steroids or other performance-enhancing drugs, including seven MVPs and thirty-one All-Stars.

PRESENT DAY What are they doing to the game I love?

9

WHY I LOVE BASEBALL

Let's be clear—I love baseball. Baseball is a great game. Maybe the greatest game ever.

I was thinking of trying to say something beautiful and poetic here, but I'll leave that to the poets. They have done and will continue to do a better job than I ever could. And I'm not into poetry. I'd much rather watch girls play volleyball. (I have a feeling more than a few of you are nodding your head in agreement.)

So I'll just say it again: I love this damn game. Always have. Always will.

Not all that long ago, I was just this wiry kid from Cuba, growing up on the streets of Miami, looking for something to do after school. And what could be easier than baseball? Couple of guys, couple of ratty gloves, an old bat (a stick if you didn't have a bat), and off you went. That feeling you got when you connected, man, it was really something.

And that's what it was about. Having a little fun. Back in those days, and even later, I wasn't thinking about all that deep stuff, about baseball *defining* America or some such thing, whatever that means. I was just a kid like any other kid, trying to be good at a game that was fun. And that's all I wanted. To be good at it. And the game gave me that opportunity.

And here's the thing about baseball: it's a democratic game. Or at least it was back then. If you can't catch, maybe you can hit. If you can't hit, maybe you can pitch. If you can't pitch, maybe they'll turn you into a good fielder. The game always seemed to try to make room for you, even if people cringed when a pop fly was headed in your direction. And if you didn't make the cut, hell, you could sit on the sidelines and cheer, which wasn't all that bad, either. Millions of American each year sit and watch the sport, so clearly there's something pleasurable about it. (Profitable, too: I heard it generated north of $5.5 billion last year.)

Maybe that's what that means, come to think of it— about the game defining America. Everyone gets a chance. You can't say basketball is America's game because it doesn't work that way. If you can't dribble, and you don't have the right genes, forget it. You're hosed. We don't want you. And much as you might like football, you're not going to make the NFL if you're built like a girl.

So really, when you think about it, baseball does sort of define what's best about this country. (And I said I wasn't going to write poetry!) Equal opportunity for all, including Cuban immigrants. All men are created equal, yada yada yada. But if you stop and think about that for a minute, it's not exactly right. All men are *not* created equal, and if you believe they are, there's something seriously wrong with you.

Some men are destined for greatness. Most aren't. End of story.

Still, when you're a kid, you're not thinking about that stuff. You're having fun. Enjoying life. And maybe, as was the case with me, you're getting more and more interested in the game. Before long, you might find yourself paying attention to things beyond your own little baseball field. For example, the day Hank Aaron beat Babe Ruth's record of 714 career home runs, I took notice. I wasn't even ten years old, but I knew it was really something. The whole country was talking about it. And every day, on baseball diamonds across America, kids were actually trying to swing like Hammerin' Hank. A black man breaks the most storied record in baseball history! Wow! And for me, a kid from an immigrant family, it was even more special. It really opened my eyes. It told me anything was possible.

Of course, years later, I found out that for months afterward Hank was deluged by letters from racist fans who hated him for breaking that record. But that's another story. I didn't think about that then because I didn't know about it. All I was thinking about was that maybe I could do that someday, and that the only thing that could stop me was me.

A few years later, another seminal moment in baseball history came during game six of the 1977 World Series. Reggie Jackson blasted three consecutive home runs on three consecutive pitches against three different Dodger pitchers! I'm a thirteen-year-old kid, playing Little League, and I actually understood what an achievement that was. And if I didn't fully understand it, I watched the replay on television, over and over, and found it absolutely electrifying every single time. I never got tired of it, and I remember thinking, *That's what I want. Yes, sir, that's for me. I want to be the guy smashing balls out of the park.* And at that moment, it wasn't just about becoming a baseball player; it was about becoming a *hitter*. That's all I wanted to be.

Years later, Cal Ripken came along, playing in 2,632 straight games over sixteen seasons. This was a guy with a good work ethic and some serious dedication to his team and the game itself. He showed up every day, ready and eager to play. He never missed a game. I used to watch him when I was a pro myself, and I'd think, "Man, what would this guy be like on steroids?"

But seriously. Those were important moments. These guys are among the immortals of baseball, and they deserve our respect. But the truth is, those aren't the moments I think about anymore. Nowadays, I think mostly about the stuff *I* did. And if that makes me seem a little self-absorbed, it's because I am a little self-absorbed, like just about everybody else on the planet. It's human nature.

I'm happy for Hammerin' Hank. I'm happy for the Bomber. And I'm happy for Iron Man Cal. But Cal played for like a thousand years, and did he hit more home runs than me? I don't think so.

And you know, honestly, when I saw what Reggie Jackson did at the 1977 World Series, I was impressed, but it was mostly about what it meant to me. And what did it mean to me? It meant that the only job worth having in baseball is being the guy who can hit them out of the park. I can't tell you offhand who the winning pitcher was in any of those World Series games. I don't know if anyone legged out a triple, and I don't remember any pretty double plays. What I do know for sure is that the home run is what got people out of their seats—*Reggie! Reggie!*—marveling at what they had just witnessed. I wanted in on that action.

When a professional player thinks about baseball, he isn't thinking about Kevin Mitchell's one-handed grab, or the 2004 World Series that ended the so-called Curse of the Bambino (unless of course you're Kevin Mitchell, or you were part of the Red Sox that year). That player is thinking about his own greatest moments, his own contributions to the sport, and if he tells you otherwise, he's a liar.

In 1988, for example, I became the first player in the game's history to hit a grand-slam home run on his first at bat in a World Series game. And by the way, that grand slam provided the setting for another memorable moment in baseball history, when Kirk Gibson, barely able to walk, stepped up the plate for the Dodgers and hit the game-winning home run. I'm glad to have been part of it, Kirk. You're welcome.

By the way, for all of Gibson's heroics—and that was definitely one of the great moments in baseball history— he needed a cortisone shot to make him feel good enough to go out there and win the game. He couldn't walk without that shot, let alone hit one out off Eckersley. By definition, that enhanced his performance. If Major League Baseball said today that cortisone shots were illegal, would we look back on his home run and say it wasn't quite as special? Would he be a cheater? Does it even matter? The fans—all the fans—got a moment to remember.

But back to me: Also in '88, I became the first player ever to hit 40 homers and steal 40 bases in the same season. Sure, I was on steroids. And sure, three guys have done the 40-40 since—Alex Rodriguez, Barry Bonds, and Alfonso Soriano—but maybe they were on steroids, too. I'm not saying they were. I'm just saying they might have been. I've already told you what I know and don't know about A-Rod and Bonds. Soriano, I have no information on, other than his spectacular performance. Why don't you ask them?

But why am I going on about them? That's not even my point. My point is that I was bringing the dying game of baseball back to life. Nobody was hitting and running like that. *Nobody.* And if you want to call me an egomaniac for spelling it out, go ahead—I don't mind. I'm all about telling the truth. Always have been, always will be.

I changed the game forever. When I got serious about playing, I introduced the fans to a new breed of superathlete: me. And then of course some clowns decided to follow me down the yellow, performance-enhanced brick road. And pretty soon most of the rest of the guys were right behind us.

Yes, I love this game. Have loved it forever. And I still remember one of the things I loved most about it as a kid, which was simply that I could actually see myself getting better. And *fast*. It's not like the actor David Carradine in *Kung Fu*, who spends twenty years trying to snatch that damn pebble out of that old bald guy's hand. I got good, and I did it fast, and it inspired me to do better. That's what baseball *is*. And that's one of the first things I loved about it.

You know another thing I love about baseball? It makes you forget. When you're out in the field, whether you're twelve years old or a seasoned vet in the majors, you're not thinking about anything except the game. If you've got an old man at home who's mean to you, what does it matter? You're outside in the fresh air, practicing hitting against a batting machine. And if you're still thinking about your mean old man, *that's* what you're doing wrong. If you're serious about the game, take it seriously. Focus.

When you get right down to it, however, the one thing I love more than anything else about baseball is hitting. You're up there, one-to-one, waiting for the pitcher to let it fly, and the only person you can depend on is yourself. That is a great feeling. Whatever comes your way, it's up to you to handle it. Nobody can help you. And you're not looking for help. This is about you, your bat, the pitch—and the swing.

And when you connect, man, there's nothing sweeter in the world. What a swing! What a sound! What a feeling. At moments like that, you think, *Here I am, where I belong.*

The next time you're at bat, you do it again. And it's always different. Always exciting. It's just you and the pitcher, and you're waiting for it, waiting to see what he's got, and more often than not what he's got isn't enough. Gotta love that.

You know what else I love about baseball? I love that that kind of hitting led to a five-year, $23.5 million contract with the Oakland Athletics, the richest baseball contract ever (back then, anyway).

And of course that led to girls, directly and indirectly. So you gotta love baseball for the girls. For the money and the girls. Ask any teenage boy what he wants in life, and those two things will be at the top of every list.

I don't need any poetry. A beautiful woman is a poem, and I love baseball for helping me understand that.

You know what else I love about baseball? I love that the home run is the one thing that matters above all else. Cal had longevity, and Roger Clemens can pitch a really good game, but where is the camera looking? The camera is looking for the home run. It's not looking for some dinky single. Dinky singles put the fans to sleep. The camera is looking at the hitter, at guys like me. And that has totally changed the sport. Why? Because the camera only cares about the hitter. ESPN and *SportsCenter* and all the rest of them, they're waiting for the big hit. Just like the fans. Because nothing compares to a hit, and delivering hits is what counts.

"That's going to be on the highlight reel tonight!"

That's what we used to say. That's what we cared about. The fans are energized by the swing of the bat, and the right swing brings them to their feet. That combination—the bat and the cameras—really changed the game. We would say, "I'm going to make the highlight reel tonight." And we weren't kidding. That was the goal, to be on the highlight reel. And that kind of thinking also changed the game. Suddenly, it was about you first, and then, almost by default, about the team. You'd come in the day after a good game, and the guys would say, "You made the highlight real last night, Jose." Or, "Saw you on *SportsCenter*."

Steroids made that happen. The highlight reel came along and you wanted to be on it, but you had to compete with the muscle and the power. And who had the muscle and the power? One guess.

Slowly but surely that changed the way we played. We began showing off. We wanted to be different. To stand out. We were part of the team, certainly, but wanted to set ourselves apart from it, too. And every year the team, and the game, suffered a little more. We wanted to be Mick Jagger, with muscles, about half a century ago, when Mick was young.

Look at me!

At one point, Nike actually turned all of this self-absorption into an amusing commercial. It featured Greg Maddux and Tom Glavine, a pair of pitchers with multiple Cy Young Awards, and our old, teary-eyed friend Mark McGwire. In the commercial, McGwire is launching massive homers during batting practice, and the crowd is going wild. At one point, Glavine, visibly frustrated, turns to look at Maddux. "How long are they going to worship this guy?" he says. Maddux studies the hot chicks, oohing and aahing over McGwire. "Hey!" he yells. "We've got Cy Young winners over here!" But it's useless. The chicks are like everybody else: they dig the long ball. By the end of the commercial, Maddux and Glavine know what they have to do: they go off to the gym to lift weights, determined to be more like McGwire.

That was a great commercial. It was funny and it was honest. The hitter—especially the power-hitter—is all that matters to the fans. Home-run hitters are the big, badass rock stars of baseball, and I loved every damn minute of it.

That's life, baby. It's about hitting the ball far, getting the fans on their feet, making the highlight reel, and going home with the money and the girls. That's what I used to do, and that's another thing I love about baseball.

10

EPILOGUE

It has been many years since I played Major League Baseball, many years since I performed on that big stage, staring down a pitcher and anxiously awaiting the pitch I could launch into the seats, but people still wonder how I fill my days. I get that question all the time. The simple answer is "My days don't need filling. They are full to overflowing."

I don't know if I have a "typical" day. I live each day as it comes, and life is always providing new and interesting opportunities. If I were to describe an average day, however, I would have to begin by admitting that I am not a morning person. Never was, never have been, never will be. I've never figured out why some people blast themselves out of bed early in the morning. The body needs rest.

So, how would an average day go? Well, I usually roll

out of bed at ten or eleven, then go off to have breakfast at Jerry's Deli. I like their eggs Benedict, but I'm not really a big food guy. I am totally not interested in food. If I could wake up in the morning and take a little pill that would constitute my nutrition for the entire day, I'd be a happy man. I think meals are time-consuming and uninteresting. I don't understand people who sit around talking about food all the time, and I certainly don't understand people who go to some fancy restaurant for the privilege of paying $100 for a steak that's about the size of my thumb. I mean, don't get me wrong: you give me a nice Cuban *pernil* with black beans and rice, maybe some fried plantains on the side, I'll enjoy it. But I can do without it. I eat to live; I don't live to eat.

I don't drink, either. From time to time, I'll have a sip of someone else's drink, and I might even indulge in a whole beer, but it's not my thing. Years ago, when I was a kid of eighteen, I found myself playing with the Pioneer League in Idaho Falls. I was living with a bunch of guys in a dump that should have been condemned—that might have been condemned, now that I think about it—but I was only making $600 a month, and it was a good deal. *Real* good, actually. My share of the rent came to $30, so I was actually able to send money home to my family in South Florida. The one thing I didn't like is that there weren't enough beds to go around, and half the time I ended up sleeping on the floor. I was young, though. I could take it.

So anyway, one night, the guys at the Animal House—

as the place was known in the community—decided they were going to get me drunk. Now, remember, I was eighteen, and I'd had a few beers in my life, and maybe an occasional sip of wine, but they were pushing the hard stuff on me, and they kept pushing: "Come on, Jose! Be a man! Have another!"

So I had another. And another. And I'm not going to get into any of the messy details, but for the next three days I was a total wreck. I finally understood the expression *sick as a dog,* because I was living it.

That was pretty much it for me and liquor. So maybe that was a good thing. Aversion therapy, I think they call it.

But seriously, the last time I had more than a single beer was during my season on *The Surreal Life,* and I already told you about my leopard-print underwear. What I neglected to tell you is that during the show I also put on women's clothes, but we're not going to talk about that brief but disturbing event in my history.

To this day, I still don't understand why anyone would want to put alcohol in their system. Even in moderate amounts, it dulls the senses, and who wants to dull the senses? Life is about being awake; about opening your eyes. Life is about being aware of everything around you, every single moment.

But I digress. Let me get back to my daily routine . . .

After breakfast, I might go for a ride on my motorcycle. I am fairly new to motorcycles. I actually discovered them in 2006, when I appeared on *The Surreal Life*. In one segment we were supposed to ride dirt bikes, and they took us to a facility for the sport. I had never been on a motorcycle in my life. I was always a car guy. Any high-end car you can name, I've probably owned it: Ferrari, Lamborghini, Bentley, Rolls—I've had them all. I even had a supercharged, nine-hundred-horsepower Porsche, which would literally throw me back in my seat when I tapped the pedal. You know those movies where you see these astronauts testing g-forces, and it's like their faces get flattened out or something, and their lips are pulled back by the intense pressure? Well, that *didn't* happen, but in my mind it felt like it might have.

The funny thing is, I'd always hated motorcycles. I hated them on principle. I didn't understand how anyone could ride around on something where one small mistake—even someone else's mistake—could cost you your life. I thought that was pretty moronic.

But the producers of *The Surreal Life* wanted to do this dirt-bike segment, so I went. We got suited up in these padded outfits, and the instructors walked us through a short lesson. This is the gas. This is the clutch. Front brake, rear brake. Yada yada yada. "Nothing to it! Just hit the gas and smile!"

I got on the bike and hit the gas and went about five feet and immediately fell over. The bike landed right on top of me, and one of the instructors hurried to my side and helped me to my feet.

"You okay?"

"Do I look okay?"

"The idea is to stay on the bike, *upright*," he said.

"Now you tell me! Why didn't you say that in the first place?"

More embarrassing things have happened. After you've had a baseball hit you in the head and go over the fence for a home run, *on national television,* you can handle pretty much anything.

I gave it another try, and before long I was actually puttering around the little track, and actually beginning to get the hang of it. I enjoyed it, too. I think I had a silly grin on my face. After about twenty minutes of riding and grinning, they figured I was ready for the Main Event, and they took me over to the dirt track. I believe it was a fairly easy course, but it had jumps on it—small ones, admittedly— and the first jump didn't like me much. I guess I caught a little air, then my front wheel landed in a muddy patch, and I went sailing over the handlebars. It felt as if I had dislocated my shoulder.

"You okay?"

"No, I'm not okay," I said.

"The idea—"

"Yeah, I know. The idea is to stay on the bike. Well, I have an idea. I'm going home. Me and bikes, it doesn't seem to be working out."

A few days later, however, I began to think about how much I'd enjoyed riding around the track, that feeling of control, and of freedom, brief as it was, and even with a silly grin on my face, and a short time later I went out and bought myself the first of several motorcycles that I would own in years to come. My favorite was a custom-made monster, eleven feet long. It was a real beauty. Two or three times a week, I'd take it into the hills above Malibu. It was truly amazing. I'd be zipping along, feeling the breezes, enjoying the fresh air and the wide-open world around me—the hills, the ocean, the sky, the clouds. It was almost surreal. It made me think of that line you always hear from Zen types, something like "It's not the goal, it's the journey." Well, I don't agree with that, not in real life, anyway, because I think you have to have goals, but it certainly works with motorcycles. It doesn't really matter where you're going because the journey is so much fun.

Riding never got tired, either. No matter how many times I rode though the same canyon, the experience was always new and fresh and different. And no matter where I was, except for maybe traffic, being on a bike gave me a terrific sense of freedom. It felt as if there were no limits, that the world was full of promise and possibility. (I know that sounds a little naive and idealistic, but the feeling only lasts till you get off the bike.)

After my ride, I would generally go to the gym. Even now, I spend at least two hours a day in the gym, every day. I do either weight training or martial arts. I am a registered black belt, in both karate and tae kwon do, and I'm also into something called Muay Thai, a form of kickboxing. I'm an expert with nunchakus, too—those Asian fighting sticks.

So, as you can see from all of this, I have a simple philosophy of life: work out hard every day, stay away from the stuff that kills you—tobacco, recreational drugs, liquor, and so on and so forth—and, at least once a day, try to get away from the world for an hour. I do that by riding a motorcycle. Some people hike. Or meditate. It all works.

After the gym, I'll eat something. I don't care what—it's all basically fuel to me—but I try to stay away from junk, and I try to get my meals over with quickly. I mean, how much do you enjoy pumping gas at the station? I'm filling the tank because I need to fill the tank, period.

When I get home, I might talk to my manager. He's always coming up with offers from reality shows:

"They want you to drive a big rig across the country."

"They want you to climb Mount McKinley."

"They want you to do a karaoke show where you only have to lip-synch."

"They're very interested in that mixed-martial-arts reality show you pitched last month."

And I always say the same thing, "Call me when we have a deal."

In the afternoon, I'll take my dog for a nice long walk, and then I might go to my acting class. (I'm still trying. Dreams die hard!)

My nights are always different. Sometimes, in the late afternoon, I'll put my daughter on the back of my bike and we'll roar off to Venice to catch the sunset. We might take a walk on the beach after, or go to a movie. At other times, we'll just hang out at home and watch TV together, which is great fun, too. I am a big fan of sci-fi horror, and of action movies, especially anything with martial arts.

Just about every other week, I attend some kind of charity event. It's easy. I show up, someone benefits. I will always support two things: kids and animals. Anything that helps kids and animals is okay in my book. I have a child of my own, of course, Josie, whom I adore, and I'm also pretty crazy about animals. In my life, I have owned everything from cockatoos to iguanas to monkeys. At the moment, though, I'm happy with my dog, Xena, a Weimaraner.

I've taken part in charity golf tournaments, charity bowling, and just-hanging-around-looking-beautiful charities, but my favorite is charity poker. I love poker, and I play serious, competitive poker. Plenty of casinos are within a short drive of my home in Los Angeles, and I am something of a regular at several of them, and of course there's always Las Vegas, just a short flight away.

One of the great things about poker is that you never play the same game twice. It's a little like riding a motorcycle through a familiar canyon and being surprised every time by all the things you missed the first hundred times you rode through it. Every player is different, and even the players you know, the guys you've played with a thousand times before, behave in unexpected and surprising ways. It really keeps you on your toes. You become a student of human nature and human behavior.

And then there are the cards, of course—your weapon. In Texas Hold 'Em, which is what I mostly like to play, each player is dealt two cards—the *hole* cards—and combines them with the community cards on the table for the best possible five-card hand. At every step, you're betting, and you're eyeballing your opponents, trying to figure out what they've got in the hole by the way they're betting and acting. There's also a lot of talk at the table, which can be telling. The guys are trying to psych each other out.

"Looks like a possible straight."

"I caught the flush on fourth street."

"Way to stay in the game with an off-suit three and eight."

"Are we here to talk, *girls,* or are we actually going to play poker?"

Sometimes, when the hand gets down to the last two players at the table, poker reminds me a little of baseball. It's just you and the other guy, the guy who's going to lose (you hope). At times like that, I feel like I used to feel when I was up to bat, waiting for the pitch, wondering what was coming and what the guy had. At the table, you wonder how much the guy has, too. He's the only guy standing between you and a pot o' money, and you're waiting for his pitch, waiting to see what he's going to do next. And here's the interesting thing: you're making all sorts of assumptions about what the guy's got in the hole based on what he's been saying, his body language, and the way he's been betting, but you never really know. And I love that aspect of the game. The not knowing. The total mystery. Because sometimes the guy has nothing. Not even a pair. And sometimes that's good enough to win the hand. Did you ever see the movie *Cool Hand Luke,* with Paul Newman? Well, you should. It's a great movie. And Paul Newman delivers a classic line about poker, with classic high style—the line that gives the movie its title. "Sometimes," he says, "nothing is a pretty cool hand."

The other thing I like about poker is the way it forces you to stay focused. It's about the goal, certainly—winning the money, whether for you or for charity—but the journey is filled with excitement.

That intensity, that type of focus, often reminds me of the best moments in baseball, and of course, the best moments in baseball are when you're standing at the plate, waiting for the pitch. You are so focused that the rest of the world doesn't exist. And when the ball comes at you, you can almost hear it, hear that whizzing sound, hear the leather groaning and straining against the seams. All your senses are heightened to an incredible degree. Then, whack! You just won the pot.

Sometimes, also, if I was at the top of my game, the ball would actually seem to slow down. Athletes call that *being in the zone*. Whenever that happened, I'd be rewarded with an extra split second—a stolen moment of time— which could make the difference between a strike and a moon shot. I loved those moments!

Poker has a similar element: occasionally, time slows down. The sounds around you become muted. The chips fly through the air in slow motion. When one of the players says something, it sounds as if he were underwater, garbled, far away. That type of thing. This only happens during the most intense moments in the game, when serious money is at stake, but there's something addictive about it, and you find yourself looking forward to those moments at the table, to that surreal, otherworldly feeling.

The other thing I love about poker is that it's really about you and your talent, nothing else. When I played ball, and I was up to bat, the team didn't even exist for me. Sure, in the back of my mind, I was doing it for the team, but I was also doing it for me. When you're out in the field, however, you go back to being part of the team, because you're working together and relying on one another to keep the other guys from scoring. But seriously, nothing beats hitting. That's really what the game is about. Maybe it's not what it's *all* about, but for me, standing in the batter's box, waiting for the pitch, that was the moment I lived and breathed for. And it's funny, because not that long ago I was describing that feeling to this guy I knew, and he told me about this family of trapeze artists, the Wallenda family. And apparently one of them, I think the father—Karl Wallenda, I believe his name was—had something really interesting to say about his chosen profession: "Being on the wire is living, the rest is waiting."

Man, think about that. *Being on the wire is living, the rest is waiting.* I couldn't have said it better. In fact, I didn't say it better. He did. And while I'm not sure I got the words exactly right, I know that the *feeling* is exactly right: hitting the ball is living, the rest is waiting.

Nowadays, with baseball behind me, I have poker. And at moments I feel like that about poker—that sort of intensity. Maybe it's unhealthy. Maybe I like the game too much. Maybe I'm even a little addicted to it. But so what? I was once addicted to hitting, and that turned out pretty well.

The last thing I'll say about poker is this: in poker, the playing field is always level. At the table, we are all equals. Size, shape, color—none of that matters and none of it means anything. It's about the cards, and the chips, and about what you can do with them. No one has an edge, and nothing can give you an edge. Not steroids, not human growth hormone—neither of which will make you a better poker player. (Not even 1 percent better.) All you've got is you and the cards and the chips and your ability to make smart choices and smart decisions. There is something almost poetic about that, though I'm not about to try my hand at poetry. (Like I said, I'd rather watch girls play volleyball.) To me, the science of the game can be summed up in a single sentence: it's about winning the most on the good hands, and losing the least on the bad hands. That's it. If you can do that consistently, you'll always be a winner. And the weird thing is, that's what *life* is like. Making the best of the good times, and figuring out a way to handle the bad.

And you know what that boils down to? Attitude. When I sit down at the table, I believe I am the best player there, and I believe I am going to win. I have to. This might strike people as delusional, and it may well *be* delusional, but it's the way I live my life.

Think about it: If I hadn't believed I could become one of the greatest baseball players of all time, I never would have accomplished what I accomplished. If I didn't think I could write a book that would blow the lid off the steroid scandal, I would have slipped into obscurity, a footnote (but a really big footnote) in the history of sports. I'm sure some people wish I *had* slipped into obscurity—A-Rod, for example—but I'm still here, and I'm going to be around for a long time to come. So deal with it.

I believe in myself. And if there are moments of doubt and pain now and then, which there are, I power through. At my core, I believe I can do anything I set myself to do, and that is what has allowed me to succeed. In my seventeen-year career as a professional baseball player, I often met exceptionally good players who were stuck in the minors, and I knew it was because they didn't believe in themselves—I knew that that was the only thing keeping them from the show.

I was the exact opposite of those guys. Early in my baseball career, I went around telling everyone that I'd have a 40-40 season. People laughed at me.

"You're crazy, man."

"Can't be done."

"Yeah, right! No one in history has done that!"

"Jose, you're dreaming."

Maybe I was dreaming, but it was an attainable dream. I *knew* it could be done, just as I knew I was going to be the guy to do it. I never once doubted myself, and that's the attitude that gets me through everything.

Nobody is going to tell me I can't do something. Nobody. And when the world tries to beat you down, you don't let it. It's that simple. You stay positive. Focused. Keep your eyes on the prize. Put on blinders. Don't look left, don't look right. The goal is right there in front of you, and that's where you need to be looking.

I was single-minded about becoming a baseball player, and it paid off. And like I said, maybe that's what it takes to succeed—that drive and that desire and that intensity. But if you want something badly enough, you'll work for it. And when you get there, you'll realize that everything you did to get there was worth it.

My daughter, Josie, will be a teenager soon. I've tried to be a good father, and I think I've succeeded more often than not, though I'm sure I come up short from time to time. Still, in one area I believe I'm actually qualified to give advice, and that concerns this business I've been talking about—this business about setting goals.

Josie, if you're reading this, please pay attention: You can do anything you want in life. *Anything*. All you have to do is figure out what you want, and who you want to be, and stay on track. It will not happen overnight, but if you believe in yourself, and you stay focused, and if every step you make is a step in the direction of that goal, even a tiny step, you will make it. *You will reach your goal.*

Along the way, people will tell you that it can't be done. That you're dreaming. That you should lower your sights and expectations. Don't listen to them. They don't know what they're talking about, and they have already been defeated by life. And never, ever, lose faith in yourself. *Keep dreaming*.

As a kid, I dreamed about baseball. And those dreams

came true. Now I'm beginning to dream my way to the next phase of my life.

Do I miss the game? Sure I miss the game. Sometimes I miss it like crazy. I thought I'd be playing baseball forever. I will never forget what Major League Baseball did to me, the way they ended my career, and I will never forgive them for it. Hell, I'd still be playing if I could. I never wanted to leave the game; the game left me.

At times I still think about what happened to me, what was done to me, and I still get angry. Then the anger passes, and for a little while I feel sad and low. But that passes, too.

At other times I think about all the good stuff that happened in my career, and I'll feel the blood rushing to the back of my throat. That's right, I admit it. I still get choked up over baseball. I think about the roaring crowds. The gorgeous stadiums. The lights, the monitors. The smell of the grass. The ball, groaning against its seams. The feel of my leather glove. The weight of the bat. Yeah, mostly I think about the bat. The weight of the bat. The feel of it in my hands.

Some nights I even dream about the game. I dream I'm still playing. I'm in the box, dug in, waiting for the pitch. I connect, a real beauty, and the crowd roars. The ball sails into the stands and a living mass of humanity moves toward it, hoping to catch a small piece of baseball history. I drop the bat, finally, and make my way around the bases, waving at the fans, who are on their feet, waving back and roaring.

And in the middle of the roar, I wake up, startled, and find myself in my bed, in my room, in my house. Alone. Not a sound anywhere. Just crushing, deafening silence. No stadium. No roaring fans. Nothing.

I drop back against the pillows, and it always takes me a while to catch my breath. It just takes it out of me, I guess—knowing it's over. Knowing it's been over for years and that I'm never going back. Ever.

After a few minutes, I'm okay again. My heart rate goes back to normal. I can breathe again.

I tell myself, "Nothing lasts forever. Not careers. Not sports records. Not life."

As I drift off to sleep again, I think about the kid I used to be, on the streets of Miami, dreaming my big dreams. And I think about my mother, and about the promise I made to her on her deathbed—a promise I kept. I became the best player I could be, and I did it in the best way I knew how, and I am proud of everything I have accomplished.

Nowadays, when I play ball with my Sunday league, I sometimes feel like I'm that little kid again. The little kid who dreamed big dreams. And sometimes, when I leave the field, when I'm driving home, I feel like I've left that little kid back there, and I miss him. Some days I don't know who I am without him, and I feel a little lost. But the feeling passes. I keep moving. Dreaming my next dream.

The game of baseball will survive the Steroid Era.

Because baseball is forever.

Poker players like to say, "The best thing about poker is

playing and winning. The second best thing is playing and losing."

Well, that's how I felt about baseball, how I *still* feel about baseball, and it's how I feel about *life*. Even when things are bad, even when you're looking at a lousy hand, you're still in the game, still on the wire, and—at the end of the day—that's what it's all about, isn't it? Living on the wire.

ACKNOWLEDGMENTS

I'd like to thank all the fans who stood by me even in the face of all the bad press that appeared when my first book, *Juiced*, was initially published. It was a trying time, but ultimately the truth prevailed. They say you find out in the worst of times who your true friends are, and when the media was trying to shout me down, the fans never wavered. So thanks for supporting me, for standing in the long lines at the book signings, for braving the cold February weather in those long lines, and for having faith in the truth of my book. I'd also like to thank my daughter, Josie, who is the love of my life. Thanks to Heidi. Thanks to Doug Ames, Rob Saunooke, and Sean Fredericks. Thanks to Pablo Fenjves for his amazing work. Thanks to Bret Saxon. Thanks to Peter Klein. Thanks to Jen Bergstrom, Tricia Boczkowski, Jen Robinson, and the rest of the team at Simon Spotlight Entertainment. And last but not least, thanks to the U.S. Congress for finally turning up the heat on Major League Baseball.

POWER STATS

BARRY BONDS	HR	RBI
1995	33	104
1996	42	129
1997	40	101
1998	37	122
1999	34	83
2000	49	106
2001	73	137
2002	46	110
2003	45	90
2004	45	101

JUAN GONZALEZ	HR	RBI
1991	27	102
1992	43	109
1993	46	118
1994	19	85
1995	27	82
1996	47	144
1997	42	131
1998	45	157
1999	39	128

MARK McGWIRE	HR	RBI
1995	39	90
1996	52	113
1997	58	123
1998	70	147
1999	65	147
2000	32	73
2001	29	64

MAGGLIO ORDONEZ	HR	RBI
1998	14	65
1999	30	117
2000	32	126
2001	31	113
2002	38	135
2003	29	99

ALEX RODRIGUEZ	HR	RBI
1996	36	123
1997	23	84
1998	42	124
1999	42	111
2000	41	132
2001	52	135
2002	57	142
2003	47	118
2004	36	106
2005	48	130
2006	35	121
2007	54	156

IVAN RODRIGUEZ	HR	RBI
1992	8	37
1993	10	66
1994	16	57
1995	12	67
1996	19	86
1997	20	77
1998	21	91
1999	35	113
2000	27	83
2001	25	65
2002	19	60
2003	16	85

(Continued)

IVAN RODRIGUEZ	HR	RBI
2004	19	86
2005	14	50
2006	13	69
2007	11	63

GARY SHEFFIELD	HR	RBI
1993	20	73
1994	27	78
1995	16	46
1996	42	120
1997	21	71
1998	22	85
1999	34	101
2000	43	109
2001	36	100
2002	25	84
2003	39	132
2004	36	121
2005	34	123

SAMMY SOSA	HR	RBI
1993	33	93
1994	25	70
1995	36	119
1996	40	100

(Continued)

SAMMY SOSA	HR	RBI
1997	36	119
1998	66	158
1999	63	141
2000	50	138
2001	64	160
2002	49	108
2003	40	103
2004	35	80
2005	14	45
2007	21	92

MIGUEL TEJADA	HR	RBI
1999	21	84
2000	30	115
2001	31	113
2002	34	131
2003	27	106
2004	34	150
2005	26	98
2006	24	100
2007	18	81

Barry Lamar Bonds

Height: 6'2"   Weight: 228   Bats: Left   Throws: Left

SEASON	TEAM	G	AB	R	H	2B	3B	HR
1986	Pit	113	413	72	92	26	3	16
1987	Pit	150	551	99	144	34	9	25
1988	Pit	144	538	97	152	30	5	24
1989	Pit	159	580	96	144	34	6	19
1990	Pit	151	519	104	156	32	3	33
1991	Pit	153	510	95	149	28	5	25
1992	Pit	140	473	109	147	36	5	34
1993	SF	159	539	129	181	38	4	46
1994	SF	112	391	89	122	18	1	37
1995	SF	144	506	109	149	30	7	33
1996	SF	158	517	122	159	27	3	42
1997	SF	159	532	123	155	26	5	40
1998	SF	156	552	120	167	44	7	37
1999	SF	102	355	91	93	20	2	34
2000	SF	143	480	129	147	28	4	49
2001	SF	153	476	129	156	32	2	73
2002	SF	143	403	117	149	31	2	46
2003	SF	130	390	111	133	22	1	45
2004	SF	147	373	129	135	27	3	45
2005	SF	14	42	8	12	1	0	5
2006	SF	130	367	74	99	23	0	26
2007	SF	126	340	75	94	14	0	28
Totals	—	2986	9847	2227	2935	601	77	762

RBI	BB	SO	SB	CS	AVG	OBP	SLG	OPS
48	65	102	36	7	.223	.330	.416	.746
59	54	88	32	10	.261	.329	.492	.821
58	72	82	17	11	.283	.368	.491	.859
58	93	93	32	10	.248	.351	.426	.777
114	93	83	52	13	.301	.406	.565	.971
116	107	73	43	13	.292	.410	.514	.924
103	127	69	39	8	.311	.456	.624	1.080
123	126	79	29	12	.336	.458	.677	1.135
81	74	43	29	9	.312	.426	.647	1.073
104	120	83	31	10	.294	.431	.577	1.008
129	151	76	40	7	.308	.461	.615	1.076
101	145	87	37	8	.291	.446	.585	1.031
122	130	92	28	12	.303	.438	.609	1.047
83	73	62	15	2	.262	.389	.617	1.006
106	117	77	11	3	.306	.440	.688	1.128
137	177	93	13	3	.328	.515	.863	1.378
110	198	47	9	2	.370	.582	.799	1.381
90	148	58	7	0	.341	.529	.749	1.278
101	232	41	6	1	.362	.609	.812	1.421
10	9	6	0	0	.286	.404	.667	1.071
77	115	51	3	0	.270	.454	.545	.999
66	132	54	5	0	.276	.480	.565	1.045
1996	2558	1539	514	141	.298	.444	.607	1.051

Juan Alberto Gonzalez

Nickname: "Juan Gone"

Height: 6'3"   Weight: 220   Bats: Right   Throws: Right

SEASON	TEAM	G	AB	R	H	2B	3B	HR
1989	Tex	24	60	6	9	3	0	1
1990	Tex	25	90	11	26	7	1	4
1991	Tex	142	545	78	144	34	1	27
1992	Tex	155	584	77	152	24	2	43
1993	Tex	140	536	105	166	33	1	46
1994	Tex	107	422	57	116	18	4	19
1995	Tex	90	352	57	104	20	2	27
1996	Tex	134	541	89	170	33	2	47
1997	Tex	133	533	87	158	24	3	42
1998	Tex	154	606	110	193	50	2	45
1999	Tex	144	562	114	183	36	1	39
2000	Det	115	461	69	133	30	2	22
2001	Cle	140	532	97	173	34	1	35
2002	Tex	70	277	38	78	21	1	8
2003	Tex	82	327	49	96	17	1	24
2004	KC	33	127	17	35	4	1	5
2005	Cle	1	1	0	0	0	0	0
Total	—	1689	6556	1061	1936	388	25	434

RBI	BB	SO	SB	CS	AVG	OBP	SLG	OPS
7	6	17	0	0	.150	.227	.250	.477
12	2	18	0	1	.289	.316	.522	.838
102	42	118	4	4	.264	.321	.479	.800
109	35	143	0	1	.260	.304	.529	.833
118	37	99	4	1	.310	.368	.632	1.000
85	30	66	6	4	.275	.330	.472	.802
82	17	66	0	0	.295	.324	.594	.918
144	45	82	2	0	.314	.368	.643	1.011
131	33	107	0	0	.296	.335	.589	.924
157	46	126	2	1	.318	.366	.630	.996
128	51	105	3	3	.326	.378	.601	.979
67	32	84	1	2	.289	.337	.505	.842
140	41	94	1	0	.325	.370	.590	.960
35	17	56	2	0	.282	.324	.451	.775
70	14	73	1	1	.294	.329	.572	.901
17	9	19	0	1	.276	.326	.441	.767
0	0	0	0	0	.000	.000	.000	.000
1404	457	1273	26	19	.295	.343	.561	.904

Mark David McGwire

Nickname: "Big Mac"

Height: 6'5"   Weight: 250   Bats: Right   Throws: Right

SEASON	TEAM	G	AB	R	H	2B	3B	HR
1986	Oak	18	53	10	10	1	0	3
1987	Oak	151	557	97	161	28	4	49
1988	Oak	155	550	87	143	22	1	32
1989	Oak	143	490	74	113	17	0	33
1990	Oak	156	523	87	123	16	0	39
1991	Oak	154	483	62	97	22	0	22
1992	Oak	139	467	87	125	22	0	42
1993	Oak	27	84	16	28	6	0	9
1994	Oak	47	135	26	34	3	0	9
1995	Oak	104	317	75	87	13	0	39
1996	Oak	130	423	104	132	21	0	52
1997	Oak	105	366	48	104	24	0	34
1997	StL	51	174	38	44	3	0	24
1998	StL	155	509	130	152	21	0	70
1999	StL	153	521	118	145	21	1	65
2000	StL	89	236	60	72	8	0	32
2001	StL	97	299	48	56	4	0	29
Total	—	1874	6187	1167	1626	252	6	583

RBI	BB	SO	SB	CS	AVG	OBP	SLG	OPS
9	4	18	0	1	.189	.259	.377	.636
118	71	131	1	1	.289	.370	.618	.988
99	76	117	0	0	.260	.352	.478	.830
95	83	94	1	1	.231	.339	.467	.806
108	110	116	2	1	.235	.370	.489	.859
75	93	116	2	1	.201	.330	.383	.713
104	90	105	0	1	.268	.385	.585	.970
24	21	19	0	1	.333	.467	.726	1.193
25	37	40	0	0	.252	.413	.474	.887
90	88	77	1	1	.274	.441	.685	1.126
113	116	112	0	0	.312	.467	.730	1.197
81	58	98	1	0	.284	.383	.628	1.011
42	43	61	2	0	.253	.411	.684	1.095
147	162	155	1	0	.299	.470	.752	1.222
147	133	141	0	0	.278	.424	.697	1.121
73	76	78	1	0	.305	.483	.746	1.229
64	56	118	0	0	.187	.316	.492	.808
1414	1317	1596	12	8	.263	.394	.588	.982

Magglio Jose Ordonez

Nickname: "Maggs"

Height: 6'0"   Weight: 215   Bats: Right   Throws: Right

SEASON	TEAM	G	AB	R	H	2B	3B	HR
1997	CWS	21	69	12	22	6	0	4
1998	CWS	145	535	70	151	25	2	14
1999	CWS	157	624	100	188	34	3	30
2000	CWS	153	588	102	185	34	3	32
2001	CWS	160	593	97	181	40	1	31
2002	CWS	153	590	116	189	47	1	38
2003	CWS	160	606	95	192	46	3	29
2004	CWS	52	202	32	59	8	2	9
2005	Det	82	305	38	92	17	0	8
2006	Det	155	593	82	177	32	1	24
2007	Det	157	595	117	216	54	0	28
Total	—	1395	5300	861	1652	343	16	247

RBI	BB	SO	SB	CS	AVG	OBP	SLG	OPS
11	2	8	1	2	.319	.338	.580	.918
65	28	53	9	7	.282	.326	.415	.741
117	47	64	13	6	.301	.349	.510	.859
126	60	64	18	4	.315	.371	.546	.917
113	70	70	25	7	.305	.382	.533	.915
135	53	77	7	5	.320	.381	.597	.978
99	57	73	9	5	.317	.380	.546	.926
37	16	22	0	2	.292	.351	.485	.836
46	30	35	0	0	.302	.359	.436	.795
104	45	87	1	4	.298	.350	.477	.827
139	76	79	4	1	.363	.434	.595	1.029
992	484	632	87	43	.312	.370	.522	.892

Alexander Emmanuel Rodriguez

Nickname: "A-Rod"

Height: 6'3"   Weight: 225   Bats: Right   Throws: Right

SEASON	TEAM	G	AB	R	H	2B	3B	HR
1994	Sea	17	54	4	11	0	0	0
1995	Sea	48	142	15	33	6	2	5
1996	Sea	146	601	141	215	54	1	36
1997	Sea	141	587	100	176	40	3	23
1998	Sea	161	686	123	213	35	5	42
1999	Sea	129	502	110	143	25	0	42
2000	Sea	148	554	134	175	34	2	41
2001	Tex	162	632	133	201	34	1	52
2002	Tex	162	624	125	187	27	2	57
2003	Tex	161	607	124	181	30	6	47
2004	NYY	155	601	112	172	24	2	36
2005	NYY	162	605	124	194	29	1	48
2006	NYY	154	572	113	166	26	1	35
2007	NYY	158	583	143	183	31	0	54
Total	—	1904	7350	1501	2250	395	26	518

RBI	BB	SO	SB	CS	AVG	OBP	SLG	OPS
2	3	20	3	0	.204	.241	.204	.445
19	6	42	4	2	.232	.264	.408	.672
123	59	104	15	4	.358	.414	.631	1.045
84	41	99	29	6	.300	.350	.496	.846
124	45	121	46	13	.310	.360	.560	.920
111	56	109	21	7	.285	.357	.586	.943
132	100	121	15	4	.316	.420	.606	1.026
135	75	131	18	3	.318	.399	.622	1.021
142	87	122	9	4	.300	.392	.623	1.015
118	87	126	17	3	.298	.396	.600	.996
106	80	131	28	4	.286	.375	.512	.887
130	91	139	21	6	.321	.421	.610	1.031
121	90	139	15	4	.290	.392	.523	.915
156	95	120	24	4	.314	.422	.645	1.067
1503	915	1524	265	64	.306	.389	.578	.967

Ivan Rodriguez

Nickname: "Pudge"

Height: 5'9"   Weight: 190   Bats: Right   Throws: Right

SEASON	TEAM	G	AB	R	H	2B	3B	HR
1991	Tex	88	280	24	74	16	0	3
1992	Tex	123	420	39	109	16	1	8
1993	Tex	137	473	56	129	28	4	10
1994	Tex	99	363	56	108	19	1	16
1995	Tex	130	492	56	149	32	2	12
1996	Tex	153	639	116	192	47	3	19
1997	Tex	150	597	98	187	34	4	20
1998	Tex	145	579	88	186	40	4	21
1999	Tex	144	600	116	199	29	1	35
2000	Tex	91	363	66	126	27	4	27
2001	Tex	111	442	70	136	24	2	25
2002	Tex	108	408	67	128	32	2	19
2003	Fla	144	511	90	152	36	3	16
2004	Det	135	527	72	176	32	2	19
2005	Det	129	504	71	139	33	5	14
2006	Det	136	547	74	164	28	4	13
2007	Det	129	502	50	141	31	3	11
Total	—	2152	8247	1209	2495	504	45	288

RBI	BB	SO	SB	CS	AVG	OBP	SLG	OPS
27	5	42	0	1	.264	.276	.354	.630
37	24	73	0	0	.260	.300	.360	.660
66	29	70	8	7	.273	.315	.412	.727
57	31	42	6	3	.298	.360	.488	.848
67	16	48	0	2	.303	.327	.449	.776
86	38	55	5	0	.300	.342	.473	.815
77	38	89	7	3	.313	.360	.484	.844
91	32	88	9	0	.321	.358	.513	.871
113	24	64	25	12	.332	.356	.558	.914
83	19	48	5	5	.347	.375	.667	1.042
65	23	73	10	3	.308	.347	.541	.888
60	25	71	5	4	.314	.353	.542	.895
85	55	92	10	6	.297	.369	.474	.843
86	41	91	7	4	.334	.383	.510	.893
50	11	93	7	3	.276	.290	.444	.734
69	26	86	8	3	.300	.332	.437	.769
63	9	96	2	2	.281	.294	.420	.714
1182	446	1221	114	58	.303	.340	.479	.819

Gary Antonian Sheffield

Nickname: "Sheff"

Height: 6'0"   Weight: 215   Bats: Right   Throws: Right

SEASON	TEAM	G	AB	R	H	2B	3B	HR
1988	Mil	24	80	12	19	1	0	4
1989	Mil	95	368	34	91	18	0	5
1990	Mil	125	487	67	143	30	1	10
1991	Mil	50	175	25	34	12	2	2
1992	SD	146	557	87	184	34	3	33
1993	SD	68	258	34	76	12	2	10
1993	Fla	72	236	33	69	8	3	10
1994	Fla	87	322	61	89	16	1	27
1995	Fla	63	213	46	69	8	0	16
1996	Fla	161	519	118	163	33	1	42
1997	Fla	135	444	86	111	22	1	21
1998	LA	90	301	52	95	16	1	16
1998	Fla	40	136	21	37	11	1	6
1999	LA	152	549	103	165	20	0	34
2000	LA	141	501	105	163	24	3	43
2001	LA	143	515	98	160	28	2	36
2002	Atl	135	492	82	151	26	0	25
2003	Atl	155	576	126	190	37	2	39
2004	NYY	154	573	117	166	30	1	36
2005	NYY	154	584	104	170	27	0	34
2006	NYY	39	151	22	45	5	0	6
2007	Det	133	494	107	131	20	1	25
Total		2362	8531	1540	2521	438	25	480

RBI	BB	SO	SB	CS	AVG	OBP	SLG	OPS
12	7	7	3	1	.238	.295	.400	.695
32	27	33	10	6	.247	.303	.337	.640
67	44	41	25	10	.294	.350	.421	.771
22	19	15	5	5	.194	.277	.320	.597
100	48	40	5	6	.330	.385	.580	.965
36	18	30	5	1	.295	.344	.473	.817
37	29	34	12	4	.292	.378	.479	.857
78	51	50	12	6	.276	.380	.584	.964
46	55	45	19	4	.324	.467	.587	1.054
120	142	66	16	9	.314	.465	.624	1.089
71	121	79	11	7	.250	.424	.446	.870
57	69	30	18	5	.316	.444	.535	.979
28	26	16	4	2	.272	.392	.500	.892
101	101	64	11	5	.301	.407	.523	.930
109	101	71	4	6	.325	.438	.643	1.081
100	94	67	10	4	.311	.417	.583	1.000
84	72	53	12	2	.307	.404	.512	.916
132	86	55	18	4	.330	.419	.604	1.023
121	92	83	5	6	.290	.393	.534	.927
123	78	76	10	2	.291	.379	.512	.891
25	13	16	5	1	.298	.355	.450	.805
75	84	71	22	5	.265	.378	.462	.840
1576	1377	1042	242	101	.296	.397	.522	.919

Samuel Kevin Sosa

Nickname: "Slammin' Sammy"

Height: 6'0"   Weight: 225   Bats: Right   Throws: Right

SEASON	TEAM	G	AB	R	H	2B	3B	HR
1989	CWS	33	99	19	27	5	0	3
1989	Tex	25	84	8	20	3	0	1
1990	CWS	153	532	72	124	26	10	15
1991	CWS	116	316	39	64	10	1	10
1992	ChC	67	262	41	68	7	2	8
1993	ChC	159	598	92	156	25	5	33
1994	ChC	105	426	59	128	17	6	25
1995	ChC	144	564	89	151	17	3	36
1996	ChC	124	498	84	136	21	2	40
1997	ChC	162	642	90	161	31	4	36
1998	ChC	159	643	134	198	20	0	66
1999	ChC	162	625	114	180	24	2	63
2000	ChC	156	604	106	193	38	1	50
2001	ChC	160	577	146	189	34	5	64
2002	ChC	150	556	122	160	19	2	49
2003	ChC	137	517	99	144	22	0	40
2004	ChC	126	478	69	121	21	0	35
2005	Bal	102	380	39	84	15	1	14
2007	Tex	114	412	53	104	24	1	21
Total	—	2354	8813	1475	2408	379	45	609

RBI	BB	SO	SB	CS	AVG	OBP	SLG	OPS
10	11	27	7	3	.273	.351	.414	.765
3	0	20	0	2	.238	.238	.310	.548
70	33	150	32	16	.233	.282	.404	.686
33	14	98	13	6	.203	.240	.335	.575
25	19	63	15	7	.260	.317	.393	.710
93	38	135	36	11	.261	.309	.485	.794
70	25	92	22	13	.300	.339	.545	.884
119	58	134	34	7	.268	.340	.500	.840
100	34	134	18	5	.273	.323	.564	.887
119	45	174	22	12	.251	.300	.480	.780
158	73	171	18	9	.308	.377	.647	1.024
141	78	171	7	8	.288	.367	.635	1.002
138	91	168	7	4	.320	.406	.634	1.040
160	116	153	0	2	.328	.437	.737	1.174
108	103	144	2	0	.288	.399	.594	.993
103	62	143	0	1	.279	.358	.553	.911
80	56	133	0	0	.253	.332	.517	.849
45	39	84	1	1	.221	.295	.376	.671
92	34	112	0	0	.252	.311	.468	.779
1667	929	2306	234	107	.273	.344	.534	.878

Miguel Odalis Tejada

Height: 5'9"   Weight: 213   Bats: Right   Throws: Right

SEASON	TEAM	G	AB	R	H	2B	3B	HR
1997	Oak	26	99	10	20	3	2	2
1998	Oak	105	365	53	85	20	1	11
1999	Oak	159	593	93	149	33	4	21
2000	Oak	160	607	105	167	32	1	30
2001	Oak	162	622	107	166	31	3	31
2002	Oak	162	662	108	204	30	0	34
2003	Oak	162	636	98	177	42	0	27
2004	Bal	162	653	107	203	40	2	34
2005	Bal	162	654	89	199	50	5	26
2006	Bal	162	648	99	214	37	0	24
2007	Bal	133	514	72	152	19	1	18
Total	—	1555	6053	941	1736	337	19	258

RBI	BB	SO	SB	CS	AVG	OBP	SLG	OPS
10	2	22	2	0	.202	.240	.333	.573
45	28	86	5	6	.233	.298	.384	.682
84	57	94	8	7	.251	.325	.427	.752
115	66	102	6	0	.275	.349	.479	.828
113	43	89	11	5	.267	.326	.476	.802
131	38	84	7	2	.308	.354	.508	.862
106	53	65	10	0	.278	.336	.472	.808
150	48	73	4	1	.311	.360	.534	.894
98	40	83	5	1	.304	.349	.515	.864
100	46	79	6	2	.330	.379	.498	.877
81	41	55	2	1	.296	.357	.442	.799
1033	462	832	66	25	.287	.344	.477	.821

William Roger Clemens

Nickname: "The Rocket"

Height: 6'4"   Weight: 235   Bats: Right   Throws: Right

SEASON	TEAM	G	GS	CG	SHO	IP	H	R	ER	HR
1984	Bos	21	20	5	1	133.1	146	67	64	13
1985	Bos	15	15	3	1	98.1	83	38	36	5
1986	Bos	33	33	10	1	254	179	77	70	21
1987	Bos	36	36	18	7	281.2	248	100	93	19
1988	Bos	35	35	14	8	264	217	93	86	17
1989	Bos	35	35	8	3	253.1	215	101	88	20
1990	Bos	31	31	7	4	228.1	193	59	49	7
1991	Bos	35	35	13	4	271.1	219	93	79	15
1992	Bos	32	32	11	5	246.2	203	80	66	11
1993	Bos	29	29	2	1	191.2	175	99	95	17
1994	Bos	24	24	3	1	170.2	124	62	54	15
1995	Bos	23	23	0	0	140	141	70	65	15
1996	Bos	34	34	6	2	242.2	216	106	98	19
1997	Tor	34	34	9	3	264	204	65	60	9
1998	Tor	33	33	5	3	234.2	169	78	69	11
1999	NYY	30	30	1	1	187.2	185	101	96	20
2000	NYY	32	32	1	0	204.1	184	96	84	26
2001	NYY	33	33	0	0	220.1	205	94	86	19
2002	NYY	29	29	0	0	180	172	94	87	18
2003	NYY	33	33	1	1	211.2	199	99	92	24
2004	Hou	33	33	0	0	214.1	169	76	71	15
2005	Hou	32	32	1	0	211.1	151	51	44	11
2006	Hou	19	19	0	0	113.1	89	34	29	7
2007	NYY	18	17	0	0	99	99	52	46	9
Total	—	709	707	118	46	4916.2	4185	1885	1707	363

BB	SO	W	L	SV	HLD	BLSV	ERA
29	126	9	4	0	0	—	4.32
37	74	7	5	0	0	—	3.30
67	238	24	4	0	0	—	2.48
83	256	20	9	0	0	—	2.97
62	291	18	12	0	0	—	2.93
93	230	17	11	0	0	—	3.13
54	209	21	6	0	0	—	1.93
65	241	18	10	0	0	—	2.62
62	208	18	11	0	0	—	2.41
67	160	11	14	0	0	—	4.46
71	168	9	7	0	0	—	2.85
60	132	10	5	0	0	—	4.18
106	257	10	13	0	0	—	3.64
68	292	21	7	0	0	—	2.05
88	271	20	6	0	0	—	2.65
90	163	14	10	0	0	—	4.60
84	188	13	8	0	0	—	3.70
72	213	20	3	0	0	—	3.51
63	192	13	6	0	0	—	4.35
58	190	17	9	0	0	—	3.91
79	218	18	4	0	0	—	2.98
62	185	13	8	0	0	—	1.87
29	102	7	6	0	0	—	2.30
31	68	6	6	0	0	—	4.18
1580	4672	354	184	0	0	—	3.13